The N

of t

Apostolic Church

From Restoration to Perfection
of the Body of Christ

GW01080819

The Nature
of the
Apostolic Church

From Restoration to Perfection
of the Body of Christ

Isaac Mwangi

MINA CHARIOTS PUBLISHERS
A division of Mina Chariots Investments
Nairobi, Kenya

© 2014 by Isaac Mwangi

Published by Mina Chariots Publishers,

A division of Mina Chariots Investments Ltd,

P.O. Box 12505-00100,

Nairobi, Kenya.

Website: www.minachariots.com

Cover design by Joseph Ngari

All rights reserved. No part of this publication may be repro-duced, stored in a retrieval system, or transmitted in any form or by any means – electronic, photocopying, recording or other-wise – without the prior written permission of the publisher. The only exception is the use of brief quotations in printed reviews and occasional page copying for personal or group bible study.

Unless otherwise stated, all scripture has been taken from the Holy Bible, Today's New International Version™ TNIV® Copyright© 2001, 2005 by International Bible Society®. All rights reserved worldwide.

Scripture marked NIV is from the New International Version®. Copyright ©1973, 1978, 1984 by International Bible Society. Used by permission of Zondervan. All rights reserved.

ISBN 978-9966-1725-3-2

DEDICATION

This book is dedicated to all the faithful who daily strive to hear the voice of the Master, focusing their singular attention on Him only and choosing to reject the many voices raised by the enemy to create confusion and lead multitudes astray, however loud those voices may be; these are the believers who have chosen to reject the hypocrisy of the established religious system, not caring about the resultant ignominy, social condemnation and persecution that is directed against them, but looking instead with hope to the day of their vindication.

And we all, who with unveiled faces contemplate the Lord's glory, are being transformed into his image with ever-increasing glory, which comes from the Lord, who is the Spirit.

(2 Corinthians 3:18)

Contents

Introduction

In the Introduction to my earlier book, *Poisoned Well of Tradition: Baptism and worthless rituals in the church*, I alluded to what I called the Father's vision. This is the vision that God has had for the church since time immemorial and seeks to have fulfilled to this very day.

I once belonged to a denomination that taught about a vision that was also called "the Father's vision." After sitting through doctrinal classes for several months to learn this vision, however, it became apparent that the vision had nothing to do with our heavenly Father. The vision belonged to the head of that branch of the sect. It was a vision designed to lift up man and to glorify a human being, all the while pretending to be serious about God's work.

That is not the sort of vision that I refer to in this book. What I call the Father's vision is not a human vision. It is nothing less than the vision of our heavenly Father about how He wants to be glorified among the people of God. It is a vision that tells us about God's burning desire to be glorified among men and the efforts He has made toward this end, including through His Son Jesus Christ. It is a vision that shows a striking unity from Genesis to Revelation in bringing about the fulfilment of God's purposes to bring glory to Himself through the elect on earth. It is a vision that begins with the perfection in the Garden of Eden and, following the fall of man, grips us with God's never-ending passion to restore all things back to that perfect state.

The Father's vision provides the guiding principles of how the church is to operate here on earth. It offers us a glimpse into the ideal situation that God in His great love has ordained for His people. It provides the rationale and the basis for every activity of the church. It tells us about how the gifts among God's people are to be used in the service of one another. It gives the boundary limits that we are to stick to, beyond which we would know we are entering dangerous territory. It helps us to be certain of the path that we take in our salvation and to recognize the nearly identical counterfeit paths laid out for us by the enemy. It helps us to avoid the snares and pitfalls laid out for us by Satan. It enables us to enjoy fellowship in love with one another. It provides a common bond of unity in the Spirit. Above all, it provides the basis for God's people to replicate the heavenly worship around the throne of God, and to shower others with the same love that God has so graciously poured upon us.

It is impossible to grasp this vision without a thorough understanding of the nature and character of God. This is because the church is meant to be the representation of God on earth. God has willed to have an extension of Himself on earth through the church, which is the body of Christ. The body sustains its life by maintaining unity with the head; if separated from its head, it becomes a lifeless form. If Christ is truly the head of any church, we must then see the life and Spirit of Christ in that church. But how can we understand what that means if we have a wrong conception of the nature of Christ's Being and Spirit? Our first and most important task must then be to go right before the throne of

God to receive a revelation of the nature and character of God, and to understand thoroughly the passion of God—His likes and dislikes, indeed His very thoughts.

If a church goes about its activities in a manner that does not display the headship of Christ, the diagnosis would have to be that either there is a spiritual malady or that this is a false church that does not derive its life from Christ at all. We would then be duty bound to give correction in the case of a true church that has gone into error, or, in the case of a false church, to expose it and seek the deliverance of those it has imprisoned.

This calls for a high level of discernment. Those whom the Lord has called and gifted to equip the saints have the divine task of listening keenly to the voice of God as He directs, rebukes, corrects and guides His church. To do so without any regard as to our own interests, personal safety or other circumstances calls for utmost surrender to the will of God. Many times the message of the Lord will cause discomfort; other times it will raise bitter opposition. Those who co-work with the Lord in the cleansing of the church must be prepared to endure ridicule, mockery, trouble and persecution. Satan and the world are set against them; the strongest opposition, however, is normally from other Christians—especially the false brethren.

Because of man's weaknesses deriving from the Fall, it may appear near impossible to achieve the high standards that the Father's vision entails. But as every parent knows, we encourage our children to aim for an A grade, even though not all of them may actually achieve that level of performance. We cannot start from a perspective of weakness and failure; on the contrary, knowing that we are guided by an Almighty God and that the prize we aim for is not an earthly certificate but eternal life itself, how much more should we aim for nothing short of the total fulfilment of God's vision for the church?

The early church did a fairly good job of living according to that vision. Whether in Jerusalem, Antioch or Corinth, the churches guided by the apostles performed superbly in the circumstances of that time. There is much that we can learn from them and encourage ourselves by looking at their example. Faced with seemingly insurmountable difficulties that included persecution, they offer us an example of perseverance and of a love for God that was so great that they were prepared to die rather than give up their faith.

After centuries of decline, it is refreshing to find Christian writers and leaders in our day who are focusing the church to look back to the early church. They are convinced that the early church as revealed in the New Testament provides God's model for His people to follow. The task, then, becomes one of rediscovering early church practices and beliefs, believing that these are normative for all Christians at all times.

But there has been no unanimity about early church practices that we need to reintroduce into the church. Some Christians have gone the whole hog and asked women to wear headscarves and remain silent during church gatherings; others have found ways of circumventing those practices that they seem to dislike. But however much a church decides to borrow from the early church, it is clear that none of them has assimilated every possible aspect of early church practice. In other words, we do not have full agreement regarding what to borrow from the early church and what to discard.

The thinking that the first century church provided the model for the church to follow was challenged in *Poisoned Well*. Even though the early church better approximated God's vision for His people than the church in our day, it by no means provided the ideal template. If our efforts at cleansing the church are focused on returning it to a model that is less than perfect, we will no doubt achieve poorer results than is the Lord's will.

To take an educationist's perspective, rather than using the script from a brilliant student who has scored 80 per cent and using it to improve a poorer student's performance, this book proposes that we look for the original marking script that will enable us to aim for a 100 per cent score. With the benefit of the teaching of the early apostles, the complete canon of scripture and the lessons of two millennia of Christianity, it is possible for the church today to rise to a higher level of spiritual attainment than did the first century church. And so it shall come to pass that the end-times church shall be filled with the glory of the Lord much more than the church of the early apostles ever did.

For this to be achieved, however, a thorough understanding of the Lord's vision is mandatory. This calls for great wisdom to sieve the wheat from the chaff. It is only by the power of the Spirit of God that the church can discern which words of the apostles portray the timeless purposes of God and which ones the time-bound circumstances of their time. Every apostolic exhortation in the New Testament must be judged by its conformity to the timeless purposes of Christ as revealed through the unity of the whole scripture. The undertaking of such an enormous and delicate task is itself an acknowledgement that the apostles were affected by their social circumstances, which coloured many of their decisions and directives.

While many churches have rushed to proclaim that they follow in the footsteps of the apostles, it is in the definition of exactly what apostolic practice entails that differences have occurred. It is my contention, however, that to pore over this matter with the aim of coming up with prescriptive church practices is to miss the instruction of scripture. A thoroughly Christocentric perspective requires that we fix our eyes wholly on Jesus; whatever it is that the apostles did or taught is to be measured against that Christological standard. The standard of the early church cannot replace the Christological standard but is itself to be judged by the latter. When this is done, it will be discovered that while the apostles did well on certain scores, they faltered in others.

13

Therefore, while their example may be worthy of emulation in certain circumstances, in others this is not the case.

The purpose of this book, then, is to explore this higher standard that Christ beckons us toward. It is a call for the end-times church to remove every spot and blemish, that Christ may find the kind of bride He desires:

> I saw the Holy City, the new Jerusalem, coming down out of heaven from God, prepared as a bride beautifully dressed for her husband... It shone with the glory of God, and its brilliance was like that of a very precious jewel, like a jasper, clear as crystal. (Revelation 21:2, 11)

In moving the church to perfection, the most important task is undoubtedly to gain a clear understanding of the nature and character of God. The church is a reflection of God, and the more accurately the church understands the Bridegroom the better it will reflect His will. The converse is also true. The reflections presented in this book may not be popular, but God's truth is never to be measured by the yardstick of popularity. Those who seek to uncover the truth must be prepared to go against established norms that hardly anybody questions, and to hold unwaveringly to the truth of the gospel that any Christological focus would unearth.

In so doing, I recognise the huge demonically-instigated wall of human tradition that prevents true worship. Those who want to be part of this movement to lift the church up to the benchmark provided by Christ Himself must selflessly offer themselves, conscious of the dust of opposition that such efforts will doubtless raise. But the time is now ripe to move the church beyond any sort of restoration that has ever been seen before. No human opposition, no demonic force, no power can possibly stop this move of the Holy Spirit.

To restore means to take something back to a previous, more

Early Fathers or this guy?
Hmmm!

useful state. But this book calls for more than that. It is not about going back to the teaching of the Church Fathers—who scored even lower than the apostles and started the descent to the Dark Ages. It is not even about going back to the first century church of the apostles. The vision in this book is for a move that goes *beyond restoration* and aims for a totally new benchmark, reaching out to the very heart of the Father and His marvellous vision for the Bride of Christ. The Father's vision is about perfecting the church.

To achieve the perfection that God desires calls for boldness to go against established norms. It takes special courage for a church leader to admit that they have been wrong all along and to set their congregation on a new course previously unknown to them. It takes grace to unquestioningly follow the leading of the Holy Spirit.

To achieve such perfection also requires us to know God intimately—for how can we become His image on earth if we do not understand Him deeply? That is why it is so critical to know the nature and character of God, which I have discussed in Chapter 3. The perspectives raised on this matter, in which I advocate a Unitarian as opposed to Trinitarian line of thinking, was something that I felt the Lord speak to me in the course of writing this book, and this was so profound that it influenced the whole direction of the book.

Private revelation departing from scripture.

My heart often goes out to the members of the congregation I once belonged to that taught a false vision of the Father. While there, I questioned the leader – whom we called "Bishop" – why he taught that tithing was commanded in the bible and yet this was not true. He was humble enough to accept my position that a proper interpretation of the texts meant that tithing was not commanded of Christians. However, he had many "buts" why he could not teach the truth. He needed money, yet even with tithing in place only a tiny fraction of the congregation gave a true tithe, so what would happen if he told the people that they

15

were free in Christ? It was disheartening listening to him deceiving believers every other Sunday thereafter that those among them who did not tithe were robbing God. It became clear that the word of God was being twisted for expediency.

When God sheds light on an issue, then, it takes much more than knowledge to move into obedience. It is virtually impossible for those who have been used to "eating the sheep" to put aside their cannibalistic instincts and instead feed the flock. Most times, it is the sheep who must shake off the chains and get away from the wolves in sheepskin. For those Christian leaders who have been teaching falsehoods out of mere ignorance and not deceitfulness, every revelation of the Father's vision should prove most welcome and refreshing. The question, "How can I admit to my congregation that I have been wrong all along?" does not arise for those who truly want to serve Christ.

It is my sincere prayer that Christians around the world will be ready to shake off every tradition that holds them back, to put aside every personal interest that prevents them from moving deeper into the things of God, and simply learn to trust the Holy Spirit's leading for the church.

Isaac Mwangi,

Nairobi, Kenya, January 2014

Chapter 1

Misunderstandings of biblical inspiration

In what way is the bible inspired? How is it God's Word? Did God put His words into the mouths of the prophets to be spoken exactly as He intended, or did He simply give them an idea and left the expression of that idea to their own individual, cultural and historical circumstances, strengths and weaknesses? In other words, are the very words inspired in themselves, or should we rather seek the evidence of inspiration in the overall message that shows the will of the Spirit displayed in the flow of narrative and poetry describing the ordinary activities of God's people?

These are weighty issues that have preoccupied the minds of bible scholars through the centuries. In grappling with these and similar questions to do with the interpretation of God's word, however, most Christian leaders and scholars have unfortunately tended to lean—to a greater or lesser extent—on looking at the actual written words on the page. The dangers in this practice will become clearer in the course of this chapter.

Moreover, inspiration does not mean that the biblical writers—including the apostles—were perfect or that they did not go into error, even serious doctrinal error. It only means that the voice of God is discernible through the writing, providing important lessons for God's people.

Many groups have accurately heard from God regarding some aspects of the church, but have failed to hear on other aspects. The difficulty in hearing God is mainly because of man's tendency to stay within a comfort zone. Humility is called for to move to any area of Christian life where the Lord wants to do correction for the perfection of His Bride. The time is now ripe, therefore, for a systematic approach to analysing the voice of the Spirit through solid, well-reasoned philosophical and biblical thinking.

Levels of reliance on the actual text (and so deception)

The extent to which Christians perceive that the literal, non-interpreted text constitutes the inspired word of God for the practice of their faith—and hence fall into deception—can be broadly categorized into several levels:

(i)   Those who claim the whole bible is literally the inspired word of God. These tend to be the most confused groups. Because it is virtually impossible to practice every possible command given to a person or group of people in both the Old and New Testaments, they will tend to practice whatever rules catch their fancy or occasional claims to illumination. Such groups may, for example, insist on keeping long hair, food laws, Sabbath observance, oppression of women and their segregation from the church gathering while on their menses, and such other unwarranted regulations.

(ii)   Those who claim to follow the New Testament, but with a selective dose of Old Testament regulations. Most Christian denominations fall in this category. The reason they seek to persuade believers to follow some Old Covenant regulations has to do with assuring their own financial support and wellbeing. They will distort the practice of the Mosaic rules that they choose to teach in order to make it possible to get financial and material assistance. Their teaching of the Old Testament focuses on tithes and offerings, which they interpret as commanding Christians to give money to their religious leaders. Apart from rules with a possibility for distortion for financial gain, they generally do not bother with the rest of the Mosaic Code and find ways of claiming that only tithes and offerings continued into the New Testament, while other rules and regulations were not commanded for all ages. The practice of early church traditions such as baptism differs widely among these groups, with some baptising by sprinkling, for instance, while others insist on immersion.

(iii)   Those who claim to follow the New Testament teaching of the early church. They follow what they perceive as the practice of the early church to varying degrees, according to their system of interpretation. Most house churches fall into this category. Having realized, correctly, that the Old Testament ended at the cross, they interpret the practice of the New Testament as necessitating as closely as possible a replication of the practice of the churches planted by the apostles. The word of God, then, becomes largely

What ?!
An appalling's bat
dispensationalist
mind-set

the word as conveyed by the apostles. Some will go to the extent of silencing women in the church gathering and obligating them to wear long dresses and headscarves. Others will insist on having a love feast at every gathering where wine (or juice) and bread must feature.

The whole of Christendom, by and large, falls into these three broad categories. And regardless of the extent to which they adore the written word, this reliance means that they are all deceived in their interpretative system.

Shortcomings of the written word

To begin with, biblical scholarship is constantly evolving. As a deeper and clearer understanding of the linguistic, historical and cultural context underpinning biblical texts is achieved, the need arises to obtain more accurate translations, leading to newer versions of the holy writ. This is in recognition of the fact that many readers are far removed—linguistically, in space and in time—from the contexts in which the biblical words were written. Thus, we may not be fully in a position to understand the nuances of meaning, wordplays and intended effect on the hearers of the original words. This, in turn, means that we may end up ascribing to a biblical text a meaning that was never intended, and that could even be impossible given the context of the time in which those words were recorded. *Overplays the MSS changes a lot; 99% of NT, known to be accurate*

Moreover, errors were expected to occur inadvertently as scribes struggled in the course of many centuries to copy the biblical text by hand. That means there may be minor variations introduced into the text because someone skipped a word or a line in a particular manuscript, or altered the punctuation, or misspelt a word, or made any other human error.

In addition, many bible versions make a point of acknowledging verses and passages of doubtful authenticity. In the gospels, for instance, these include Mark 16:9-20 and John 7:53-8:11. How can we be sure that such passages in the Bible are really God's word? Where there is doubt, many scholars agree that the relevant passages can only be used for the purpose of mutual edification, but it would be misleading to use them for any doctrinal teaching.

But even more disturbing is the fact that scripture has through the centuries been deliberately corrupted by people all too keen to prove certain theological perspectives right. The Roman Catholic Church, for instance, changed the word "churches" to read "church" in the epistles so as to make the bible conform to its teaching that it was the only true church, as in 1 Corinthians 11:16 in the Douay-Rheims Bible. *That's really not a serious error → hard to accuse RC of deliberate*

Similarly, 1 John 5:7 was altered in the King James Version to *tampering here* support the doctrine of the Trinity. More recent versions have rectified this anomaly, as the following comparison with Today's New International Version shows:

> For there are three that bear record in heaven, the Father, the Word, and the Holy Ghost: and these three are one. And there are three that bear witness in earth, the Spirit, and the water, and the blood: and these three agree in one. (1 John 5:7-8, KJV)

> For there are three that testify: the Spirit, the water and the blood; and the three are in agreement. (1 John 5:7-8, TNIV)

While the corruption of the above verses has been easily identified by scholars, other instances may not be so easily detectable, meaning that millions of believers could be holding to doctrinal errors that they defend as "God's truth" owing to the corruption of scripture by unscrupulous church leaders in ages past, *hold a* especially the Church Fathers. This leads us to question the very *serious dogma*

21

integrity of scripture, meaning that believers must learn to lean more on the principle of love—and sheer common sense—than on the written word as a tool for guidance. *Hardly. We do the work a can trust the work and*

Again, a close scrutiny of many bible versions will reveal notes *be hvest about trying on* with alternative renderings of verses. Some of these renderings *prove* may differ significantly from the main text, raising difficulties about what God is really speaking and obviously creating room for confusion. What, then, one believes to be God's word from such verses could be highly subjective and completely wrong from what the Spirit actually intended.

A study of Romans 8:28 from the later editions of the New International Version and Today's New International Version can serve to explain this point fully. Three renderings of this verse are provided, beginning with the main text:

1. And we know that in all things God works for the good of those who love him, who have been called according to his purpose.

2. And we know that all things work together for good to those who love God, who have been called according to his purpose.

3. And we know that in all things God works together with those who love him to bring about what is good—with those who have been called according to his purpose.

The obvious question that arises is: What did God really say? Do *Him* all these renderings mean the same thing? Of course they don't! *point dea*

Starting with the first rendering, the implication in this verse is *It hasn't* that God works for the good of only those who love Him. But *By Nah* this goes contrary to scripture, because it would mean God's goodness to us is dependent on our goodness toward Him. But

22

is He not faithful even when we are faithless, giving his rain and sunshine to the righteous and the wicked alike (2 Timothy 1:13, Matthew 5:44-48)? If we believe God is good to everyone all the time, so much that He even sent His own Son to those who were His enemies, it would follow that the first rendering of this verse presents an obvious problem since it ascribes to God a character that is contrary to the perfection scripture teaches.

The second rendering encourages a superstitious mind-set, one that does not give glory to God: Things will simply work out on their own, somehow they will. It fails to recognize that it is God who is working behind the scenes to make those things work for good. Moreover, apart from spiritual truths and eternal salvation, it is not true that things will always work together for good. When personal or national tragedy strikes, how does this fit into a good plan? It is a verse many people in trouble falsely cling to, urged on by their spiritual leaders.

But even worse is a consideration that this rendering implies that God is behind evil. Yes, God is bringing sickness, death, tragedy and evil upon you so that He can bring about some good out of it, this rendering appears to state. That brings us back to an examination of the nature and character of God, where we find that He is not responsible for calamity. He comes to give us life, while Satan comes to kill, to steal and to destroy (John 10:10).

I am convinced that the third rendering gives the most accurate and correct perspective. God is looking for people to partner with in bringing about His will—through prayer, carrying one another's burdens, compassion for the less fortunate, generosity, and whichever other way. He does not work alone as the first rendering implies, and neither will things just fall in place like a jigsaw puzzle as the second rendering seems to suggest. No, God is seeking to partner with you to do good to that neighbour in trouble, if only you can listen to his voice and do as He tells you. Some scholars have in fact argued that the Greek New Testament supports this view of "working together", saying the verb used here is the same as that used, for example, in the letter of James for faith and works "working together" (James 2:22).

It is unfortunate that this third rendering of Romans 8:28 is buried in the footnotes rather than being part of the main text. All the same, our study of this verse illustrates the point that what we call scripture is quite often heavily distorted and does not faithfully convey the meaning intended by Christ.

When anyone points to a biblical passage to support whatever argument, all these dangers are never far away. The expectation is normally that because the biblical text represents the very words of God, all argument ceases and the matter being contended is established. But considering all the points mentioned above, we shouldn't be too sure that what we read represents, on the face of it, the very word of God.

Moreover, most times other texts to counter any argument can readily be found—biblical texts, in other words, can be used to support almost any and every point of view.

That's not what happens

Additionally, because these texts are always evolving as biblical scholarship advances, how is anyone to be sure that God's will is properly encapsulated in the words on the page of any text referred to? Since God's word stands forever, it is not His word that would be changing but our deficient understanding of that word. If we acknowledge that we do not even have the original texts written by the apostles and the prophets, we cannot begin pretending that inspiration lies in the very words themselves.

No two languages are fully translatable one into the other in every respect. There will be tongue-twisters that once translated do not convey the same effect in any language other than the original; poetry that loses its metred flow and double meaning; and narrative that is so conditioned on an understanding of a particular cultural milieu that the reader who is removed from that culture and language will first need a course on the language, history and geography of a people before he can begin to appreciate that piece of literature.

Because God's word is eternal, it follows that it is above human culture. No language or tradition can accurately and fully express the will of a God who is beyond human comprehension and therefore linguistic expression. But because we serve a loving God who wishes to constantly reveal Himself to imperfect beings, He finds a way of showing us the little of Him that our languages, cultures and frail understanding will permit. The mental picture that this leads to is obviously imperfect and can hardly qualify to be authoritatively called "the word of God," being only a miniscule fraction of the divine glory—a polluted and diminished image of the perfect God.

Take, for instance, the very concept that Jesus is the "Son of God." What does this really mean? Jesus was simply the visible expression of the one eternal God, the Father. The words "Father" and "Son" are therefore not to be confused with their normal usage among humans. But in order to get to our level of understanding, Jesus used a term, "Son," that we are familiar with. Of course, this term may not communicate the fullness of the meaning God intended to convey.

If we accept, then, that individual words, passages and books in the bible do not at the fundamental level represent the unchangeable, perfect will and purposes of God, but rather these as filtered through the prophet's own understanding or as simplified for the ease of understanding of the hearers, we can then begin to appreciate the challenges involved in correctly discerning God's word. It is easy to confuse a writer's weakness, prejudice or cultural conditioning as representing God's will, and this error has tainted Christian theology and practice since the days of the early church. It is also quite possible to take what has been simplified into human terms for ease of understanding and wrongly assume that this is indeed the reality of God's word.

An All-Encompassing Understanding

How are we to avoid such mistakes as these? One important measure is to seek to gain an overall understanding of the bible and God's will as revealed from Genesis to Revelation. This sort of bird's eye view, once acquired, then becomes a yardstick for discerning what really is of God and what isn't, or why God is represented in a particular way in a certain book and how that depiction is right or wrong.

By so doing, we do not fall into the trap of blindly following and believing whatever is written on the page, but become judges of those words, guided by God's Spirit. Having acquired an over-arching understanding of the nature and character of God, we can then approach specific biblical texts with this understanding.

This is exactly why the bible exhorts us to be constantly "fixing our eyes on Jesus" (Hebrews 12:2). If we take the words of Moses, or Isaiah, or Paul, and elevate them to the status of words coming out of the mouth of God, would we not by that very fact have stopped fixing our eyes on Jesus and taken our gaze else-where? We do not get the word of God by looking for what Paul said and agreeing with him, lifting up his words and thoughts as a standard in biblical study and debate; no, we get to God's word by looking at what the apostle said and then discerning what the Spirit says about that which Paul said.

It is absolutely essential, then, for any Christian who wants to walk in the Spirit to learn how to tell God's truth, from which the varieties of men's interpretations as revealed in the bible can be seen. Our task should never be to identify with any particular saint's interpretation and run with it, but on the contrary to as-sess how much of the truth had been revealed to that person and their obedience to it. From that, we gain comfort and encouragement that we who have received a much fuller illumination can persevere and be equally victorious, while avoiding the mistakes of these predecessors in the faith.

Whenever an individual text does not agree with our overarching understanding, our task is to investigate the reasons why that is so, but not to change the overall understanding that informs our interpretation. This is not to say that our basis for interpretation—the overall understanding—cannot be deficient, but only to affirm that it cannot be nullified by individual texts or books that appear to go contrary to that understanding. Any correction to the basis of an interpretation that was obtained through systematic study of the whole of scripture to come up with what the Spirit is saying can only arise out of a similar "train of thought" showing the progressive working of God's Spirit with a thread that runs from Genesis to Revelation, from the Old Covenant to the New Covenant.

An example or two will serve to illustrate this point. Our overriding understanding tells us that the love of God for us is infinite and all-embracing, and that He wants His people to love one another with this same passion. Because of this great love for one another, human barriers crumble and Paul can confidently declare:

> There is neither Jew nor Gentile, neither slave nor free, neither male nor female, for you are all one in Christ Jesus. (Galatians 3:28)

Having thus established this high standard, we find the same Paul elsewhere urging slaves to obey their masters and for these masters to be considerate of their slaves (Ephesians 6:5-9, Colossians 3:22-4:1). The question is: Since Paul was writing his letters to born-again believers, what happened that he should lower the standard in these texts to tolerate master-slave relationships among them? *Basic interpretation.*
Equality of status "in Christ";
reality of roles continue

If we were to accept that inspiration lies at the level of individual words and thoughts, then we would have no option but to accept that slavery is acceptable before God, and therefore slaves must be obedient to their masters. These masters are only called upon to be fair-minded in their dealings with their slaves.

When we rise above this to a level where we interrogate scripture itself using a higher vision granted by God through a holistic understanding of scripture, then it becomes clear that slavery has no place in the church. We then realize that Paul's words, or those of any writer that do not measure up to the divine standard, are the result of either or both of two possibilities: that the writer did not have a complete illumination and understanding of the matter, or that he was reacting to local situations and circumstances, in the process shining the light of Christ the best he could in those circumstances. We would be wide off the mark to assume that the situation described, say acceptance of slavemaster relationships in this instance, shows us the inspired will of God.

Isn't it quite obvious that someone who loves another cannot put that person in bondage? It is then easy to judge: Between those who as recently as in apartheid South Africa supported the enslavement of others using biblical texts, and those like William Wilberforce who were vehemently opposed to the slave trade, who really had heard from God?

The Letter and the Spirit

Again though, he's read that in. Speaking into doesn't equal approval

The letter, then, tells us that slavery is fine, but the Spirit finds slavery abhorrent. The letter says women should be silent in church, but the Spirit tells us to encourage the participation of everyone in the full life of the people of God. Many churches will restrict women to participation in singing and giving testimonies; but no, what is required is the full participation of women in each and every activity of the church, including declaring what God may be speaking through scripture.

People who insist on following the text of the written word may want to ponder Paul's words:

> He has made us competent as ministers of a new covenant—not of the letter but of the Spirit; for the letter kills, but the Spirit gives life. (2 Corinthians 3:6)

The difference is simple. Following the letter means looking at a specific verse or passage and demanding unequivocal obedience to what is written. In following the Spirit, however, we study any verse from two levels. First, we examine the full context in which those words were spoken to see whom they were spoken to and why this was so. Second, we seek to put those words within the overall message of scripture, seeing the development of the thought described in those words and how this fits within the plan of salvation and redemption. It is only then that it can be decided whether those words are applicable as they are to a specific person or audience, or whether they are intended to teach us completely different lessons but are not meant for a simplistic and direct application by today's believer. Where the words do not agree with the message of the rest of scripture, questions of the integrity of the biblical text also arise and should be pursued vigorously.

The tendency to look at the letter without seeking the Spirit is behind a large number of false teachings that have left many believers in total bondage.

For instance, many pastors and believers will quote Malachi 3:8-10 to justify tithing. They will also quote Paul's words about giving generously to ask believers to give church leaders money and possessions. Yet, a careful study of the context will obviously show that the words in Malachi were not meant for new covenant believers. The context of 2 Corinthians 9:6-7 shows that Paul wrote these words for the purpose of exhorting believers to give generously to assist the brethren in Jerusalem who were going through hard times, not for himself to do as he wished with the funds raised. Such facts are rarely if ever mentioned, and ignorant believers will be made to believe that God is demanding that they give their money to this person standing before them at the pulpit. That is a grand deception.

Studying the context, then, is sufficient for a believer to know exactly who God is speaking to and why, and from there to take the next step of discerning how this may or may not apply to their own lives. Sometimes, however, matters become more complicated and one would have to literally move outside the bible, while still following the Spirit as revealed in scripture.

The written word is simply a springboard to get to the Spirit, with no additional value. It is a roadmap for those who have been chosen to inherit salvation to get to Jesus. Contained in the written word, hidden from ordinary human knowledge and requiring God's illumination for anyone to understand, are instructions about how to hear Jesus speak: real gems of wisdom about the kingdom of God. It is not the word at face value that brings joy, since the written word is in itself lifeless, but the One to whom the word points. When we allow the enemy to sow confusion and make us stop at the level of the word, whether in the Old or the New Testament, we fail to see Jesus and to hear from Him. Yet, there are good reasons why the more one turns to the Old Testament, the greater their deception will be.

The Old versus the New Testament

The bible describes several covenants—or agreements with various peoples or groups—that God made. These include the covenants with Noah and Abraham. But it is the covenant given to Moses that is best known and dominates the Old Testament books.

Although a covenant represents an agreement, in actual fact it is God who dictates the terms of the covenants He makes. While the bible narrates the story of God's dealings with various people in the Old Testament who placed their faith in Him and the covenants He entered into with them, nowhere is it mentioned that we are to follow those covenants ourselves. Indeed, the New Testament makes it clear that Christians are under the new covenant initiated with the blood of Jesus at Calvary. In that case, the Old Testament is important as the history of our salvation and for edification purposes, but it cannot be used as a source of teaching for Christian practice.

Moreover, Christ said that He had come to fulfil the Law and the Prophets, which were but foreshadowing Him. The New Testament therefore contains the revelation of the fullness of Christ, who was merely seen in types and shadows in the Old Testament. In fact, the book of Hebrews says directly that the New Testament is superior to the Old Testament (see, for instance, Hebrews 7:18-19, 22, and 8:6).

These considerations mean that Christians have no business re-enacting Old Testament rituals and practices. It is worth remembering that Christ lived under the Law, and that the new covenant began only at His death; rituals and practices that persisted in His time and that He may have participated in or appeared to give His approval of are, therefore, all to be considered abolished after the cross.

In other words, the teaching about what the church ought to do is to be sought in the period after Christ went up into heaven and poured out the promised Holy Spirit. Thus, the epistles occupy primacy of place in discerning the will of God, even above the gospels.

To use an analogy, in the Old Testament God was speaking to children, and at the level that children would understand Him. In the gospels, they are now adolescents and have a little more

Forgets the gospels written after the Epistles

understanding. Maturity comes with the outpouring of the Spirit, and He deals with them as people who can now eat the meat of the word. We gain a clearer understanding of God, therefore, when we examine His dealings with the mature rather than the children and adolescents.

To take an example of tithes and offerings, these were observed with great reverence in the Old Testament. Then Jesus came and said that justice, mercy and faithfulness were more important. He even alluded that making peace with a brother was more important before God than giving an offering at the altar. When we study the lives of the apostles and their writings, we find that they simply asked for generosity, and tithes and offerings were no more since these belonged to an order that had ended (Hebrews 9:15). The light shed on an issue, therefore, increases progressively through the bible, and it would be a deceptive throwback to take a teaching given at the childhood or adolescent stage and hold on to it as the ultimate truth from God.

Apostolic shortcomings

But even the word from the apostles cannot be taken as the unerring word from God. Even though they showed significantly greater light than any other group before them, the apostles were still encumbered by cultural practices that had nothing to do with following Christ. In certain situations, this even caused conflict among them, as was the case when Paul confronted Peter at Antioch (Galatians 2: 11-14).

Under inspiration of the Holy Spirit, the apostles enunciated ideals that we see they themselves did not fully live up to. The human weaknesses that prevented the realization of those ideals do not nullify the ideals themselves. We ought to have the wisdom to focus the church on the ideals and to sieve out the imperfect practice of the apostles.

The examples of this human disconnect between ideal and practice are many. For instance, Paul says there is neither male nor female in the church, yet goes ahead to place restrictions on women. He tells the Romans to always bless even their enemies, yet he tells the Corinthians to hand over a believer to Satan! (1 Corinthians 5:4-5). Forgiveness is put forward as a virtue, but we see Paul failing to practice this in dealing with Mark (Acts 15:36-40).

When it came to Jewish ritual practices, this failure is quite pronounced. Paul did himself at one time give in to pressure from the Jews to undergo ritual washing in an attempt to pacify them (Acts 21:20-26). The practice and the teaching of the apostles therefore displayed the greater light they had received mixed up with their own Jewish background, beliefs and practices.

This is why, in *Poisoned Well*, I argued against the tendency by undiscerning Christians to take up Jewish customs while confusing these for Christian practice. These non-binding practices of the apostles included baptism, anointing with oil, special hours of prayer and temple worship. Great Compulsion anyone ?!

Moreover, even though the apostles displayed a much greater understanding of God's will than the Old Testament prophets, they were still grossly deficient in this respect. Due to human weaknesses, no person can possibly give the word of God with absolute accuracy, though elements of God's truth would be traceable in a godly person's words. As such, a close scrutiny will reveal that even the ideals the apostles expounded were often tainted.

Of course, the apostles only had the canon of the Old Testament to rely on. Today, we are more fortunate in that we have the complete revelation of the Old and New Testaments. We therefore have much greater light to enable us to see where the apostles went wrong, and it would be foolish to simply follow their example blindly.

Consider the following passage in Paul's letter to the Romans, for instance:

> Therefore God gave them over in the sinful desires of their hearts to sexual impurity for the degrading of their bodies with one another. They exchanged the truth of God for a lie, and worshipped and served created things rather than the Creator—who is forever praised. Amen.

> Because of this, God gave them over to shameful lusts. Even their women exchanged natural relations for unnatural ones. In the same way the men also abandoned natural relations with women and were inflamed with lust for one another. Men committed indecent acts with other men, and received in themselves the due penalty for their perversion.

> Furthermore, since they did not think it worthwhile to retain the knowledge of God, he gave them over to a depraved mind, to do what ought not to be done. (Romans 1:24-28, NIV)

The image of God that comes out of this passage is heavily influenced by Old Testament thinking of the character of God. It is a throwback to the fearful, vengeful, and fire-breathing God of the Old Testament. But we know from our knowledge of the complete scriptures that we serve a merciful God who desires that the whole world may be saved. Christ came for sinners of every kind, without distinction. He is patient in waiting for sinners to come to repentance, and watches over them in the hope that they will repent. He does not hand them over to Satan. It is the devil who lures them deeper into sin, taking advantage of the fact that sinners have invited him by their refusal to accept God's salvation. God is forever good and cannot lead anybody to temptation and sin as Paul appears to suggest above (see James 1:13-14).

An understanding of the word of God that transcends the de-

34

ficiencies of individual writers and cultural considerations can enable a believer to sit as a judge and determine to what degree an apostolic or other writing is in agreement with the word of God. In doing so, we recognize our own weaknesses, but utilize the gifts God has given us and remain as objective as possible in our assessment of how much a passage or book of scripture has conformed to what the Spirit is saying.

Moreover, in order not to misunderstand a writer, it is often profitable to look at the overall message that a writer is delivering rather than trying to press a point of view by looking at specific details. Examine the following passage, for example:

> They devoted themselves to the apostles' teaching and to the fellowship, to the breaking of bread and to prayer. Everyone was filled with awe, and many wonders and miraculous signs were done by the apostles. All the believers were together and had everything in common. Selling their possessions and goods, they gave to anyone as he had need. Every day they continued to meet together in the temple courts. They broke bread in their homes and ate together with glad and sincere hearts. And the Lord added to their number daily those who were being saved. (Acts 2: 42-47, NIV)

Many churches have used this and similar passages to justify taking one form of bread or another as part of their worship during church gatherings. Others have used it to justify using titles such as "Apostle" for the leader. Yet others have used it to justify building programmes that have oppressed their followers at the expense of helping the poor among them. But does this passage really teach all these things?

Anyone with a basic sense of comprehension can see that Luke was simply describing the love and joy of the early Christian community. He was not laying down doctrines about church buildings, titles, rituals of bread or other such matters. If one is keen to prove any of these doctrines to support their sectarian perspective, they would need to look for passages that speak into these matters—if at all they will find any.

Using a verse to support something that was only mentioned in passing and was never the subject matter being addressed can sometimes lead one to a minefield of contradictions. A good example can be found by looking at the book of Revelation. House churches, because they do not (quite correctly) believe in putting up physical structures for worship, often use this verse to support their position:

> I did not see a temple in the city, because the Lord God Almighty and the Lamb are its temple. (Revelation 21:22)

John was simply describing the vision he saw, not giving a treatise on why it is not right to put up temples for Jesus. Indeed, this verse can be countered by numerous verses in the same book where a temple in heaven is mentioned, such as Revelation 14:17 and 15:5-6. The point, then, is that we can only prove something from a passage if that passage was indeed intended to prove that point.

Tracing a writer's walk with God

Many Christians make the fundamental error of thinking that the biblical account of any writer or group of writers was written with the same level of revelation. This mistake then prevents them from growing in their faith beyond the level of that writer at that point in time, or they end up confused when they come across passages—even by the same writer—that seem to contradict each other.

But the spiritual walk is a painstaking journey for all those who embark on it—including the prophets and apostles who wrote scripture. They grew in their faith gradually, and to understand them we must be ready to discern this growth and the changing perspectives that went along with it.

Solomon is a good example from the Old Testament. Despite his famed wisdom, this great king was living in sin and revelry by the time he wrote the book of Ecclesiastes. His tainted wisdom is clearly evident to the discerning reader. He begins by writing about the hopelessness of life, yet we know that those who have fixed their eyes on the Lord are always talking about the great hope that they have—not hopelessness.

In his warped wisdom, Solomon says that "what is twisted cannot be straightened" (Ecclesiastes 2:15). This contrasts sharply with the words of someone in the Spirit such as John the Baptist, who declared that, "The crooked roads shall become straight, the rough ways smooth" (Luke 3:5).

There are important lessons the Holy Spirit would teach us by reading Ecclesiastes, including how the gifts of God—wisdom in the case of Solomon—become distorted when we stop relying on Him fully as the source of our spiritual lives. But if we assume that the wisdom of Solomon remained unaffected by his lifestyle and that his books reflect the timeless wisdom of God, we would end up with wrong interpretations and beliefs.

In the New Testament, the lives of the apostles reflect this same variance in inspirational wisdom at various stages of their lives. Fortunately, this generally reflects growth, unlike in the case of Solomon where there was retardation and even regression. A couple of examples will sufficiently illustrate the growth in spiritual understanding by the apostles.

In the book of Acts, there are numerous cases narrated of water baptisms, which were done by immersion soon after believing the message of the apostles. Yet, Paul later writes derisively about this practice, saying that Christ did not send him to baptize but to preach the gospel (1 Corinthians 1:17). Peter is even more dismissive of water baptism, telling his readers that the baptism he was concerned about was "not the removal of dirt from the body" (1 Peter 3:21). *How do you get Peter being dismissive from that?!*

Why would Paul and Peter be insulting a practice that they warmly embraced in the earlier days of their faith as narrated in the Acts of the Apostles? The answer has to do with the spiritual growth and understanding of these apostles over time. But when we assume that the apostles received the full revelation of the gospel in an instant and did not experience growth the way all other Christians do, then we end up sometimes accepting teachings and practices that they adopted before they reached real maturity. Whereas it would appear that they later outgrew their earlier beliefs concerning water baptism, it becomes impossible for later Christians to reach the same understanding if they do not follow the progression of these apostles' thinking, accepting that their writings showed specific levels of growth.

A further example has to do with blessing and cursing. Paul understood that evil came from Satan, who is the enemy of God and His people. Yet, He shows lack of understanding that there can be no cooperation with such an enemy by handing over a believer to Satan (1 Corinthians 5:4-5). His later writings show greater understanding, exhorting believers that they were to bless and never curse (Romans 12:17-21). Christians who do not follow the progression of the apostle's growth will have no qualms of conscience praying for Satan to afflict other believers, *Have he* with whom they may have disagreed, following in the example *even* of Paul. Clearly, this is wrong, and a study of the progression *read the* of Paul's thinking shows he outgrew that attitude, just like he *passage?* outgrew water baptism.

The task of discerning the spiritual growth of the apostles is made particularly difficult by the fact that the epistles are not ordered chronologically in the bible. One therefore has to read between the lines and in relation to other epistles to discern what book was written before the other.

Reading specific verses and passages as complete in themselves and capable of providing an accurate interpretation of God's word leads to the error described here. One of the things a good student of the word ought to do is to get a wholesome picture of a writer's thinking—including the progression of the writer's thoughts over time. That makes it imperative that when we read scripture, we should always have at the back of our minds the question, "What was this writer's understanding at this particular time and did he later revise that understanding and, if so, why did he do so and in what manner?" It is only by so doing that we can confidently say that Paul, Peter or any other writer teaches a particular perspective on an issue.

It is always the case that people are associated with the latest stand that they have held on an issue, while previous positions can only be mentioned as a part of their history. It would therefore be inaccurate to state without any qualification that Paul teaches Christians to call upon Satan for help in disciplining errant Christians, or that Paul and Peter supported water baptism. Though these statements would hold true of certain stages in their spiritual growth, they cannot be touted as representing Paul's or Peter's thinking when it can be shown that the perspectives of these apostles later changed. And this approach to interpretation needs to be increasingly applied if we are to hope to get to a true understanding of the teaching of any biblical writer or of the early apostles.

Comparison with other texts

It is quite common for people to draw support for their arguments from specific words or details in a passage without caring much about the big picture in the passage or book of scripture. This inevitably leads to conclusions that are unsupported by the weight of evidence. Where such conclusions are biblically sound, this is more the result of coincidence than due to any force of correct argument, since the premises would not have been valid in the first place.

The best way to approach interpretation is by asking the question: What point is the writer striving to prove by this passage? Once this question is answered, then we know that the rest of the details of the story are coincidental and were not intended to prove any point separate from what the writer or speaker intended.

As an example, we can consider the passage where Jesus said, "Anyone who speaks against the Holy Spirit will not be forgiven, either in this age or in the age to come" (Matthew 12:32). The overall message has to do with blasphemy of the Spirit, which the context shows to be an attribution of the things of God as belonging to the devil. Jesus was refuting accusations that He was using the power of Satan to drive out demons.

But can this verse also be used to make the point that there is forgiveness of sins in the next world? This was not the matter Jesus was teaching in this passage, and from a reading of other scriptures we get the context of the whole scripture, from which we can say it is not possible for sins to be forgiven in the next world: We are told that there is "a great chasm" between the two kingdoms that would not have enabled the rich man to receive any help from Lazarus (Luke 16:31).

Because of conveniently ignoring other relevant scriptures and not putting into the context of the whole scripture the phrase regarding forgiveness of sins "either in this age or in the age to come", the Roman Catholic Church has the unfortunate teaching that it is possible for sins to be forgiven after death. This is what lies behind their rituals of masses for the dead, indulgences, and the doctrine of purgatory. These sorts of mistakes are not limited to this denomination, however, and permeate the whole of Christendom.

Moving beyond the written text

One cannot come to the conclusion that slavery is an ungodly and evil practice based on any one passage in the bible: You must move beyond it, but still being in accord with what God's Spirit is saying in scripture. That marks the difference between a legalist and one who is truly in the Spirit. A legalist will want every statement elaborated with reference to a verse. One who is in the Spirit, however, only needs to discern the direction the wind of the Spirit is blowing on an issue, and can then move in that Spirit well beyond any situation described specifically in the bible. Sometimes, as in the case of slavery, he may even appear to be going in opposition to the written word. That means he may not be able to prove the correctness of his actions by quoting scripture, but can only do so by carefully analysing overall trends of the hidden working of the Spirit in scripture.

The reasoning described in the matter of slavery as discussed here can be applied to many other areas where the church has been held in bondage. One important area, of course, concerns the place of women in the home and the life of the church. A logical consideration of this matter, using the same parameters used to argue against slavery, means that no woman should view herself as lower than men in any respect due to her gender. There is absolutely no reason—save demonic interference—for women to be prevented from doing anything in the life of the church or held to be subservient to men in any manner whatsoever.

Women are not less of God's children than men, nor are their prayers any less powerful than those of men. Christ did not die for men a little more than He did for women. Yet an interpretative system that focuses on specific verses rather than the overall thrust of God's Spirit ends up putting half of Christendom in bondage, just as for hundreds of years it encouraged the trans-Atlantic slave trade.

From specific verses that speak of a lack of distinction in the church, and the many that exhort us to love one another, we can come to the conclusion that our love for all humanity and all brethren cannot allow us to cripple half of those who come to Christ, demanding that they should shut up rather than exercise their spiritual gifts.

But the stumbling block of specific verses prohibiting women from full communion remains and cannot be ignored. Where this sort of conflict is apparent, it is worth remembering that we are called upon to follow the Spirit and not the letter.

Rather than picking on verses to selfishly put women or other races in bondage, we can use our over-riding focus of love to discount anything that goes contrary to it. We can also study the move of the Spirit on an issue over time, and thus correctly discern God's will in that matter.

Trends described in progressive revelation of God's Spirit

A patient study of any topic through scripture reveals riches that one can never get through a rushed approach, or by listening to others and believing whatever they tell you. This means studying with the aid of a concordance, a topical bible and other materials.

Take again the issue of slavery as an example. Slavery did not arise out of God's command, but is the result of men's imperfections as they sought power and dominance over each other. When we follow the story of God's dealing with His people right from the Old Testament, we find Him seeking freedom for them. After Joseph was sold into slavery and later went into prison, God finally got him out. Later, he freed the Israelites from bondage in Egypt, and commanded them to similarly be considerate of slaves and to avail themselves of the opportunity to set them free:

> If any of your people, men or women, sell themselves to you and serve you six years, in the seventh year you must let them go free. And when you release them, do not send them away empty-handed. Supply them liberally from your flock, your threshing floor and your winepress. Give to them as the Lord your God has blessed you. Remember that you were slaves in Egypt and the Lord your God redeemed you. That is why I give you this command today. (Deuteronomy 15: 12-15)

In the writings of the prophets, we again find God comforting those who were unfortunate enough to be slaves and even eunuchs—assuring them that He loved them and had good plans for them:

> For this is what the Lord says:
>
> "To the eunuchs who keep my Sabbaths,
>
> who choose what pleases me
>
> and hold fast to my covenant—
>
> to them I will give within my temple and its walls
>
> a memorial and a name
>
> better than sons and daughters;
>
> I will give them an everlasting name that will endure forever. (Isaiah 56:4-5)

In the New Testament, Paul finally makes the famous statement that there is neither slave nor free in the church (Galatians 3:28). The Spirit, we can clearly discern, is on the side of freedom. God will work within a cultural context to better the lot of slaves where slavery exists, but that is not to be equated with an approval of that abhorrent practice. And going by this discernment,

So why does he assume Paul does? And why equate slavery with sacred commodities?

we can proceed with the Spirit to move beyond Paul's writings and state that we have an obligation not to merely seek fair treatment for slaves, but absolute freedom and restitution.

Christ came to redeem us from our bondages, not to enslave us further. When this progressive approach to discern the move of the Spirit through scripture is applied to issues of women empowerment, it becomes clear that the word of God is very liberating and nobody should think of how to make women shut up at a church gathering. The Spirit of God is a Spirit of redemption: In any area of our human experience, we will never go wrong when we seek rights and freedoms for groups and minorities suffering any kind of prejudice or ill-treatment. That does not mean everything such a group does must be right, but that we should not be oppressive and unfair in our dealings because of our own different experience, or simply because our values don't agree with theirs.

Chapter 2

Conceptions of God–partial and imperfect

The bible gives a record of how men have thought of God over time. With the coming of the New Testament, there was a dramatic change in perceptions from those that were held in the Old Testament. A failure to understand that God as reflected in the bible reflects merely a writer's understanding has made many Christians to wonder at the difference between the "cruel" God of the Old Testament and the loving Father of the New Testament. Some sects have even taught that these are two different Gods.

Because God is so full of love, He often does not upset our erroneous belief systems, especially where a correction would result in unnecessary emotional or social turmoil. But whoever seeks to know Him better, He says, shall surely find Him.

Even though there are traces of truth in our conceptions and knowledge of God, the fact is that these are less than perfect. In the Old Testament, the conceptions of God were farther away from the truth than in the New Testament. Understanding this situation enables us to grasp the message of the ancient writers of both the Old and New Testaments without holding on to any false conceptions as if these were divine truth.

It is vitally important to understand the character of God if we are to avoid confusing Him with Satan, which is what the devil loves most so that He can get the glory. In scripture, this confusion is clear where things are attributed to God that properly belong to Satan. An example was given in the last chapter, where Paul told the Romans in his letter that God had driven sinners into sexual impurity, shameful lusts and a depraved mind. A few more examples of such blunders that confuse God with Satan will be given in this chapter.

Old Testament Conceptions of God

When we examine what is said of God in the Old Testament, we find the image of a God who can hardly be loved: One who kills and destroys, is demanding and difficult to please, looks for the slightest opportunity to bring calamity, punishes every act of disobedience, and is generally quite distant even from the people He claims to love.

Why didn't God make the effort to correct these impressions? Every father knows the opinion young children have of their fathers: that they know everything, are powerful and can get for them whatever they need. Why don't fathers bother to correct their four-year-olds on such matters? The answer is obviously that such young children have not reached a level of understanding that would permit any useful correction. The same applies to our dealings with God—even today, your level of maturity determines how God deals with you.

This is why the New Testament uses symbolisms of slaves and

children to explain the relationship between the Law of Moses and Christianity:

> What I am saying is that as long as the heir is a child, he is no different from a slave, although he owns the whole estate. He is subject to guardians and trustees until the time set by his father. So also, when we were children, we were in slavery under the basic principles of the world. But when the time had fully come, God sent his Son, born of a woman, born under law, that we might receive the full rights of sons. (Galatians 4: 1-5)

Paul goes on, in the same chapter of Galatians quoted here, to compare the old and new covenants with Hagar and Rebecca, respectively. He ends up encouraging his readers that they were not children of the slave woman but, like Isaac, were children of the free woman. And if Paul's comparison is to be advanced even further to its logical conclusion, then it means the thinking obtained from the covenant of Mount Sinai (in childhood and slavery) has to go now that we have reached maturity and freedom.

A journey through some sections of the Old Testament will show how immature conceptions of God affected the people's views about God; these childhood views continue to hold Christendom in bondage to this day.

The account of the Fall

Following the sin committed by Adam and Eve, God readily proclaims judgment, declaring the curses that must befall Satan, the woman and the man (Genesis 3: 14-19). Thus the image is entrenched of a God full of wrath, without mercy, cursing and bringing evil upon men who transgress his laws in any manner.

Like a father talks to his children without explaining all the details, God had simply asked Adam and Eve not to eat of the tree of the knowledge of good and evil. Once they ate of the tree, He again told them the consequences, once more with hardly any details of how these would come about. The logical thing for Adam and his wife would be to think that God was responsible for what befell them, and this is what other children (spiritually, that is) have assumed to this day.

From our knowledge of the New Testament, we know that God does not curse. He even tells his followers not to curse, but to always love even their enemies (Matthew 5:43-48; Romans 12:14). Because we also know that God is the same yesterday, today and forever (Hebrews 13:8), it would obviously baffle anyone why God would himself curse while asking others not to do the same.

But the answer is simple. Because He was dealing with small children having little understanding, God did not tell Adam and Eve that they had given Satan a foothold. He did not tell them that Satan would be the one afflicting them, now that they had decided to partner with the devil. Painful as it was for God to see His children stray into Satan's territory, it was much more loving to keep from them the fact that they were now at Satan's mercy.

What would be the consequences for Adam and Eve? The woman would experience pain in childbearing, and we know millions of women have died throughout the ages while giving birth. Yet, our God is the giver of life and not a killer.

God also told the woman that the husband would rule over her. Again, this did not represent a God-ordained order. God was simply describing life in the fallen state. Those whose minds are far from Christ try to dominate other people in their quest for money and power; because women are physically weaker than men, they are easily dominated and men "rule over" them.

Even the physical earth feels the effects of the Fall, and Adam is told that he will have to toil painfully, all the while contending with thorns and thistles. If anyone believes that the circumstances described in Genesis 3 describe a God-ordained situation, they should oppose modern agricultural methods and any attempt to control weeds. But if we find it profitable to control weeds despite the curses spoken against Adam, there is no reason why we should not similarly fight the curses spoken against the woman. That means seeking the emancipation of women from all forms of bondage, as well as doing our best to ease the pain women go through in childbirth by ensuring suitable and hygienic facilities. When we don't, we partner with Satan to oppress our fellow humanity while thinking we are doing it for God.

The Exodus and Giving of the Law to Moses

When Moses was called by God as he approached the burning bush (Exodus 3), he was asked not to move any closer and to remove his sandals, "for the place where you are standing is holy ground." This enhances the impression that God is not freely approachable and our physical appearance or dressing matters to Him. It also gives people the idea that there are holy places.

But it must be remembered that the Old Testament was simply a shadow of the New Testament. God, who at the time of Moses simply gave his identity as "I am who I am," has now come in human form to dwell among us and reveal Himself more fully. Many Christians are deceived by focusing on the canon of Old Testament texts without seeking an understanding of how Jesus has brought to us a much fuller revelation of God.

The plagues that were brought upon the Egyptians, far from causing the Israelites to love God the more, actually made them even more fearful of this dreadful God. At the giving of the Law, when Moses saw the disobedience of the people and the golden calf they had made, he made the Levites to go through the camp killing their own people, "and that day about three thousand of the people died" (Exodus 32:28). More such punishments were to follow as the Israelites time and again fell into disobedience as they travelled through the wilderness. There was absolutely no mercy.

Indeed, the Law handed over to them with all the accompanying regulations was nothing but a string of do's and don'ts, with specified punishments for every act of disobedience. To please God, one had to do or fail to do a whole lot of things. It is virtually impossible for anyone to obey all these laws to the letter. This is why Paul writes that "the law was added so that the trespass might increase" (Romans 5:20). He also says that "sin, seizing the opportunity afforded by the commandment, deceived me, and through the commandment put me to death" (Romans 7:11).

The Law of Moses, then, did not bring life. God remained a distant figure who was known more for punishing than saving. That is why even the Israelites were so fearful that they told Moses they did not want to move near their God, but that he (Moses) should do that on their behalf (Exodus 20:18-19). Christians who focus on the Old Testament and insist on recreating the order of the Old Testament as represented by the Ten Commandments, the priesthood, rituals and other circumstances cannot enjoy the life of Christ. They remain in the shadows, fearful and deceived.

The Books of Poetry, Wisdom and Prophets

Is it any surprise, considering all the facts mentioned so far in this chapter, that the people in the Old Testament would tremble with fear and avoid any contact with their God, believing that this would lead to certain death? Their relationship with God was not based on love but fear. That explains why, in all his supposed wisdom, Solomon advised his subjects that, "The fear of the Lord is the beginning of knowledge."

Due to their low level of revelation, the Old Testament saints commonly attributed the things of Satan to God. They thought that God was behind all activities, including calamities, and this obviously increased their dread tremendously. A good example is the book of Job.

While the story of Job begins with a conversation in heaven that attributes the evils that befell Job on Satan, the narrative shows that the latter had to first get permission from God to afflict Job. That raises questions about God's goodness, for why would he allow sickness and death to come upon His servant for no reason at all? Eventually, therefore, the buck stops with God. In fact, this is exactly what Job said in his moment of sorrow:

> "Naked I came from my mother's womb,
>
> and naked I will depart.
>
> The Lord gave and the Lord has taken away;
>
> may the name of the Lord be praised." (Job 1:21)

Throughout the book, the idea is entrenched that God "hedges in" people (Job 3:23), destroys trouble makers and makes them perish in his anger (4:8-9), goes about wounding and injuring people (5:18), and unleashes terror (6:4). God also wrongs people in many ways (19:6-12), strikes people (19:21) and does many other horrible things.

With this kind of Old Testament worldview, it is not surprising that David sees any calamity befalling those who do not love God as "the punishment of the wicked" (Psalm 91:8). The insinuation, of course, is that God is the one who inflicts this punishment. He is a God who can be called upon to "pay back to the proud what they deserve" (Psalm 94:2) and to "slay the wicked" (Psalm 139:19).

But it is not only upon the wicked that the Lord brings down disaster. Even on His own people, whenever they go astray, he causes calamity time and again:

> "Therefore, this is what the Lord God Almighty, the God of Israel, says: 'Listen! I am going to bring on Ju-

dah and on everyone living in Jerusalem every disaster I pronounced against them. I spoke to them, but they did not listen; I called to them, but they did not answer.'"
(Jeremiah 35:17)

This type of outlook probably explains why, to this day, all sorts of calamities are attributed to God. Wherever there is sickness and death, destructive earthquakes, road accidents and other calamities, people will readily declare that the matter was God's will, or an act of God. Yet, the New Testament has now revealed that it is the devil who comes to kill, to steal and to destroy (John 10:10).

In addition, the predominant thinking in the Old Testament was that one had to do something in order to make God happy and be in His good books. It was all about offering sacrifices, observing Sabbaths, and many other external rituals and ceremonies.

In fact, through the prophets of the Old Testament we sometimes get a glimpse of God's own view regarding the Law. The prophets at times emphasized the spiritual aspects of a right relationship with God and frowned upon legalistic obedience to the law handed down through Moses (see, for instance, Psalm 51:16-17 and Isaiah 66:1-4).The prophets looked forward to the coming of Christ and the initiation of a new covenant. It would be a different covenant from the burdensome one that they had where sins had to be continuously repented and endless sacrifices of animals offered:

> "The time is coming,"
>
> declares the Lord,
>
> "when I will make a new covenant
>
> with the house of Israel
>
> and with the house of Judah.

It will not be like the covenant

I made with their forefathers...

"This is the covenant I will make with the house of Israel

after that time," declares the Lord.

"I will put my law in their minds

and write it on their hearts.

I will be their God,

and they will be my people.

No longer will a man teach his neighbour,

or a man his brother,

saying, 'Know the Lord,'

because they will all know me,

from the least of them to the greatest,"

declares the Lord.

"For I will forgive their wickedness

And will remember their sins no more." (Jeremiah 31:31-34)

Despite such glimpses of light, however, the predominant outlook among the prophets remains one of fear of God and his destructive power. The Law of Moses remained the code by which people related to God, and the work of the prophets was largely to tell people where they had gone wrong in departing from the Law given to them. Again and again, they would ask them to fulfil what was expected of them as per the law. That explains the exhortations to observe such things as Sabbaths (Isaiah 58:13-14), tithes (Malachi 3:8-12) and animal sacrifices (Malachi 1:10-14).

When Christ finally brought us the new covenant, He did say that this new wine would be destroyed if consumed in old wineskins (Mark 2:21-22). As can be seen, the Old Testament practices and conceptions of God that are still so prevalent in our day are actually harmful and were never intended to be carried over into the New Testament era.

New Testament Conceptions of God

While the New Testament canon throws much greater light on the nature and character of God than does the Old Testament, it is in no way perfect or exhaustive. Actually, the conceptions of God in the New Testament books can be separated into at least two distinct parts: the Gospels and the Apostolic era.

Conceptions of God in the Gospels

Many Christians wrongly assume that the gospels contain a higher level of truth than the rest of the bible, for the simple reason that these books describe the life of Jesus Christ. This is why many bibles will even have the words of Christ in red ink, believing that these words hold the revelation of God in its fullest extent.

The truth is quite different. The gospels rank higher than the Old Testament books, but certainly lower than the epistles in terms of Christian teaching and practice. They offer a sort of transition period from the old to the new covenant, and anyone basing their Christian practice mainly on the gospels will experience significant confusion.

This is because although the gospels are found in the New Testament, in terms of dispensation they belong more to the Old Testament. Christ was born under the Law, and it is only at the cross that He ushers in the New Covenant (or testament). John the Baptist, the one who came to prepare the way, was the last of the Old Testament-style prophets, even though his record is in the New Testament books.

Yet, the gospels are profoundly different from the Old Testament books. Christ the light of the world has come, but there is so much darkness that He would blind everyone if He shone His light all at once. In His love, He shines a significant amount of light among people accustomed to life under the shadows of the law. He grants them a new dawn and lifts them up into some kind of spiritual adolescence, but admits that full knowledge of the truth will have to wait a little longer (John 14:26).

Just as God spoke to people at the level of their understanding in the Old Testament, He does the same in the gospels. There is a much greater illumination of issues, but the overall picture is still grossly deficient.

The Old Testament was concerned with outer rituals and ceremonies. Man had to do or not do a string of actions to please God. In the New Testament, however, we know that salvation is by the grace of God through merely believing in Jesus Christ— no rituals are necessary, and neither are there rules and regulations to be kept. God has done everything for us, and our appropriate response can only be to give him continual, spontaneous sacrifices of praise and thanksgiving.

When we look at the gospels, however, we find that Jesus charted a middle path between these two extremes of rituals against no rituals, actions versus grace. In fact, by relying only on the evidence of the gospels, it would be somewhat difficult to know what rituals the Lord would approve of and what he would discard. He told the Pharisees to be more concerned with justice, mercy and faithfulness, but not to neglect the outward practice of tithing. He taught His disciples to pray directly to their Father who hears in secret, yet sent those he healed to the priests to perform the sacrifices commanded by Moses—and by so doing gave tacit approval of the mediatory role of the Levitical priesthood and of animal sacrifices.

Jesus told His disciples that all they needed to be victorious and bear much fruit was to remain in Him, yet still tolerated practices like fasting, appearing to take it for granted that His disciples were supposed to fast. He did not tell them the truth that this ancient practice was of no value in the kingdom, since all that matters is to be in Christ; food does not make us any better or worse off, as the apostle Paul so clearly stated (Romans 14:17, 1 Corinthians 8:8).

Today, we are no longer required to do many of these things that Jesus gave His approval for during His ministry on earth. That means believers must depart from the actual teachings of the earthly Jesus as described in the gospels and seek an apostolic interpretation of the events of the Lord's lifetime on earth. This underlines the fact that spiritual maturity was not gained at the time of Jesus as captured in the gospels, but rather with the outpouring of the Holy Spirit—who came to teach in a way that the apostles, who were previously "dull of hearing," would comprehend the message from God much more clearly.

Today, the Holy Spirit continues this same work, moving us even beyond the understanding the apostles ever achieved, but in the same spirit of love and freedom. That is why we are able to oppose slavery rather than ask slaves to obey their masters, and we declare women free to participate in the life of the church despite Paul's concerns. That's all apostolic reinterpretation of the events of Jesus' time and of the epistles of Paul.

Christ is the one who appoints apostles, giving them the message they will deliver from His heavenly throne to the church of their day. We need therefore to move away from the earthly Jesus in order to reach the heavenly Jesus: The former is but a stepping stone to get to the latter.

The earthly Jesus was constrained by the cultural limits of the people He revealed Himself to; the heavenly Jesus speaks abstract truths that the church should aim to achieve despite the shackles of local circumstances. The earthly Jesus spoke to people who did not have the Holy Spirit as an ever-present help to enable them gain real knowledge of God; the heavenly Jesus dwells in our midst through the Spirit and speaks to us day by day. The earthly Jesus was interested in charting a middle way that would be acceptable to the hearers and attract them to a clearer understanding of God beyond the Judaism of their day; the heavenly Jesus pours out gems of wisdom and knowledge from his throne without measure, and only our individual refusal to accept the truth becomes a limiting factor.

The historical Jesus took upon Himself human weaknesses and was subject to hunger, tears, pain and death. Having emerged victorious from the grave and ascended into heaven, the exalted Christ is not subject to any of these weaknesses. That is why we who are in Him are able to mock death and ask, "Where, O death, is your victory? Where, O death, is your sting?" (1 Corinthians 15:55).

The earthly Jesus dwelt among men in a fallen material world; the heavenly Jesus, however, is to be found in the spiritual realm, where He dwells in unapproachable light in total perfection—no idolaters, murderers, thieves, adulterers, or anything impure can come near Him.

The earthly Jesus may have given concessions for some rituals of His day, but the heavenly Jesus wants us to move beyond this level of understanding. For sure, there are practices described in the gospels where there is hardly any debate that these are Old Testament practices and not required of Christians. The circumcision of Jesus, the purification of Mary, and animal sacrifices described in the gospels are examples of such practices. But so are baptism—a ritual washing—and tithing.

In the gospels, Jesus teaches in a way that shatters the standards of the day. In Matthew 5, for instance, he gives radically different views about murder, adultery, divorce, taking oaths, and revenge. He also goes against the Sabbath laws.

In talking about these issues, Jesus drives attention from external appearances to internal purity. But only to a point, for the person whose brother has something against him will still have to return to this physical altar to offer sacrifices (Matthew 5:24).

Jesus declares that He has come to fulfil the Law (Matthew 5:17), but does not openly state that this fulfilment entailed an abolition of that very Law (Ephesians 2:15). He says He will rebuild the temple in three days—even at one point prophesying its destruction—but does not say that the physical temple was merely a shadow of something better and that the real temple will now be the people of God (1 Corinthians 3:16-17). Jesus spoke this way because His hearers would not have fully understood Him at the time, leaving greater illumination to come through the mouths of the apostles.

Even in his teaching, Jesus used examples drawn from the existential experience of the people. He gave parables using slaves and masters that would have resonated with the people of His time, yet that should not be taken as a tacit approval of such relationships. It is only later that the apostle Paul—having obviously listened carefully to the heavenly Jesus—declares that in Jesus' kingdom there is neither Jew nor Gentile, slave nor free, male nor female.

Knowing the simplicity of the people and how hard it was for them to understand His message, Jesus withheld from them the complete truth on a lot of issues. He told them to pray to their Father in heaven, yet we know God is everywhere. Since by their understanding God was responsible for both good and evil, he told them to pray to Him not to lead them into temptation, yet we know God does not tempt and neither can He be tempted (James 1:13). He even said that God will forgive them their sins on condition they also forgave others when they wronged them, thus appearing to make God's love conditional upon our actions (Matthew 6:14-15); we know, however, that He remains faithful even when we are faithless (2 Timothy 2:13).

The Jesus the church ought to listen to is no longer the Suffering Servant on earth, but the King of Kings and Lord of Lords who reigns from heaven. Jesus does not want His Bride to cast herself according to the imperfect image of the God revealed in the gospels, but rather to train her eyes to gaze steadily at the heavenly Christ, who is the epitome of heavenly glory, purity and holiness. Christ wants a bride without blemish, one who reflects the glory of God; to reach that state, the church must have a clear idea of the God it is supposed to mirror. It is to this higher standard of perfection that Jesus beckons His church to aspire. And that is why He continues to speak to us from heaven (Hebrews 12:25).

There is no contradiction between the earthly and the heavenly Jesus. The earthly Jesus brought grace and truth in a limited form; the heavenly Jesus pours out even more of this grace and truth. As believers, we fix our eyes not on the earthly Jesus described in the gospels, but on the heavenly Christ who is seated on the throne of heaven in all His glory and power, far above all rule and authority, power and dominion, and every name that can be invoked, surrounded by all the heavenly host.

Whenever we hear people tell others that Jesus says this or that, the issue that should concern believers is, Which Jesus—the heavenly Jesus or the earthly, historical Jesus? While we should not neglect to study what is written about the historical Jesus, our preoccupation in the interpretation of God's word has to do with what the heavenly Jesus is saying, recognizing that it is only by so doing that we will gain the fullness of revelation.

Now, the question then becomes, how do we get to know what the heavenly Jesus is saying? This is achieved through apostolic interpretation, which is the reason God has given gifts to His people (Ephesians 4:7-13). True apostolic power is soft power, quite unlike that seen on television throughout the world as false apostles seek followers. True apostleship is about persuasive authority exercised through accurately dividing the word of God and speaking forth His very words and desires for the church. This heartbeat of God can only be discerned through spending time in the Spirit, and yet the heavenly Jesus is the Spirit (2 Corinthians 3:17-18).

What is the impression of God that arises from the teachings of Jesus in the gospels? On the one hand, this is a God breaking away from the Old Testament conceptions, and yet not fully. On the other hand, He is a God who displays grace, but again with some limits. It is the image of a God experiencing transformation: He offers forgiveness, but only on condition you forgive others; He wants direct fellowship with His people, yet they must still retain the intermediary ministry of the Levitical priesthood; He desires a people who will worship Him neither on the mountain nor in Jerusalem but in spirit and in truth, yet still considers the temple in Jerusalem the House of Prayer; and He declares that He desires inner purity rather than an outward show, but still requires tithes and animal offerings.

This is a God who is giving and yet holding back. It is a God who desires to love and be loved, yet still invoking fearful thoughts in the minds of people. It is a God who wants multitudes to move to a true knowledge of Him, yet stops short of revealing Himself fully so as not to create confusion among people for whom that truth would be too upsetting. This is a God who therefore purposes to reveal Himself in a restricted manner in the gospels— much more substantially than He had ever done before, but still stopping short of shedding too much light until the coming of the promised Holy Spirit.

Christians relying on the limited revelation of God given in the gospels will, for sure, end up seeking God based on a false understanding of His nature and character, thus relating with Him in a highly defective manner. Such believers will limit themselves to the earthly Jesus, yet the Lord wants us to break free from Jewish and other human inhibitions so as to relate with Him according to His elevated position of authority and dominion.

Conceptions of God in the Apostolic Era

The apostles have been variously described as interpreters of the Jesus event. Following the death, resurrection and ascension into heaven of their Master, they received the promised Holy Spirit (John 14:26) to teach them and remind them of all that Jesus had said. They went about reinterpreting the events of the Old Testament in the light of the coming of Jesus, and the meaning of things that had taken place when the Lord was physically in the world now became clearer. It is therefore by looking at the apostolic activities and writings that we get a much better conception of God than can be obtained in the Old Testament or the gospels.

The apostles correctly discerned that we serve a God of love. This love, Paul said, was so great that nothing could possibly separate us from it (Romans 8:38-39). It is such a distinguishing characteristic of God that it could even be said that "God is love" (1 John 4:16b). In fact, whatever benefits they enjoyed, the apostles recognized that, "Every good and perfect gift is from above, coming down from the Father of the heavenly lights" (James 1:17).

In this respect, the apostles were vastly different from the Old Testament prophets. Their writings were mainly exhortatory, urging believers to love one another in response to the great love that had been showered upon them by God through sending His Son into the world. This loving God was always in their midst, with all of them serving as a royal priesthood, and the apostolic teaching was to enable believers to flow with what the Spirit of God was doing among them. This was of course a great departure from the prophetic writings, where the people were simply told what the Lord was saying but were not called upon to become participants in the priesthood.

In a radical departure from Judaism, the apostles also taught that it was not because of our actions that we merit God's favour and salvation, but that this was simply out of God's grace arising from His goodness (Ephesians 2:8-9). The Law, therefore, could not save man and had been put in place to direct its adherents to Christ, who came and fulfilled the Law before finally abolishing it at the cross (Ephesians 2:14-15).

But despite all what can be said to their credit, the apostles still erred in their conceptions of God, encumbered by Judaic presumptions that had proved too difficult to demolish. In Chapter 1, it was demonstrated how Romans 1:24-28 gives the image of a fearful God full of wrath. This image is buttressed by the following verses also, among others:

> Then the church throughout Judea, Galilee and Samaria enjoyed a time of peace. It was strengthened; and encouraged by the Holy Spirit, it grew in numbers, living in the fear of the Lord. (Acts 9:31)

> Show proper respect to everyone: Love the brotherhood of believers, fear God, honor the king. (1 Peter 2:17)

But fear is not of God, who progressively shows in scripture that He wants His children to draw closer to Him in love and not fear. As the apostle John correctly wrote, perfect love casts out all fear (1 John 4:17-18). Because of fear, believers cannot enjoy fellowship with God. They are instead preoccupied with misplaced thoughts about things they think they can do to please Him and ward off His wrath—tithes, first fruits, Sunday services, constant repentance prayers, and a host of other activities.

Yet, the bible is categorical that salvation is only by grace through faith in Jesus Christ. Regarding fear, the writer to the Hebrews says:

> Since the children have flesh and blood, he too shared in their humanity so that by his death he might destroy him who holds the power of death—that is, the devil—and free those who all their lives were held in slavery by their fear of death. (Hebrews 2:14-15)

Sin causes spiritual death, which these verses teach Christ has overcome on behalf of all believers. People fear physical death because they have no certainty about what happens thereafter, and will especially fear eternal torment in hell. By his death and resurrection, Christ displayed His power over death. Moreover, he has taken over our sins and fully atoned for them, so that we should have no fear arising from our sins and the punishment that these deserve.

That is to say that we can go before God and enjoy true fellowship unhindered by any sin, since this barrier has been taken away. We can speak to God and praise him regardless of our human weaknesses, since no man can ever be perfect in thought and action. That doesn't mean we should encourage sin in our lives, but it means that whatever sins may be there are no longer an obstacle in approaching our God, since He even remembers them no more (Hebrews 8:12).

In that case, repeated repentance means we do not believe that Christ has really done all this for us. We keep on reminding God of something He says He no longer remembers—and therefore should never be a factor in our relationship with Him. A believer in constant repentance is yet to be freed from fear of spiritual and even physical death. For such a person, Christ died in vain since such prayers show that the believer is no better than his Old Testament predecessors.

In that case, we find that John, too, erred by requiring born-again believers to go into repentance. In the messages to the seven churches in Revelation 2 and 3, he leaves no doubt that the believers ought to repent, or else they would face certain unpleasant consequences. These messages not only instil fear, they move the believers back into a continuous mode of repentance reminiscent of the Old Testament.

In fact, John goes ahead to suggest matters that show a complete Jewish mentality that has little to do with Christ. He talks of "a synagogue of Satan" (Revelation 2:9, 3:9), for example, giving the idea that God in the New Testament cares about synagogues. He even implies that eating food sacrificed to idols is wrong (Revelation 2:14); this conflicts with the teaching of Paul, who seemed to have received a much greater light in this matter (1 Corinthians 8:7-8).

To his credit, the writer to the Hebrews does not instil fear and stop there. He shows by His writing that he seeks to influence his readers to act positively through certain fearful messages, but almost immediately reassures them that they are not subjects of wrath (Hebrews 6:4ff, 10:29ff). A much better way, of course, would be to exhort people to actions of love and purity without having to scare them first. John excels in doing this in his gospel and letters, and it is surprising that he regresses into projecting a scary semi-Jewish worldview in the book of Revelation.

It is also worth noting that there are issues where the apostles in fact appeared to regress in their teaching to even below the level taught in the gospels. While exhorting the Corinthians to give generously, for instance, we find Paul going overboard to the point of being manipulative. He first tells the Corinthians about the giving of the Macedonian churches, of course with the intended effect that the former would want to match that sort of giving. He goes on to say that he wants to test the sincerity of their love by comparing it with the earnestness of others (2 Corinthians 8:1-8). While generous giving is to be encouraged, we should leave the Holy Spirit to speak to people about their own giving without burdening them with thoughts about how they should reach the level of others (as though it were some sort of competition), recognizing that circumstances may be different for various people and churches.

Paul also exerts more direct pressure on the Corinthians, telling them that he had been boasting to the Macedonians about the Corinthians' promise to assist, the implication being that he would not want to be disappointed. He starts at this point being concerned about maintaining appearances to others rather than simply allowing the Corinthians to give without undue pressure:

> For I know your eagerness to help, and I have been boasting about it to the Macedonians, telling them that since last year you in Achaia were ready to give; and your enthusiasm has stirred most of them to action. But I am sending the brothers in order that our boasting about you in this matter should not prove hollow, but that you may be ready, as I said you would be. For if any Macedonians come with me and find you unprepared, we—not to say anything about you—would be ashamed of having been so confident.

In addition, Paul tells the Corinthians that greater giving would result in more abundance. Now, what could possibly be more manipulative than that? Enticing people with promises makes them give with hearts full of the expectation that they will receive some greater personal benefit from God in return. While he correctly tells his readers that nobody should give out of compulsion, therefore, he actually plants a seed of compulsion and manipulation of the Corinthians!

God's provision flows out of His abundant grace, not our own efforts whereby we try to compel Him to grant greater provision by giving out something. Such giving cannot be said to come out of a generous heart, but is merely an investment. Neither does God's goodness depend on our own goodness, in this case generosity. God remains good all the time, providing for our needs even when we have been unfaithful. And He asks that we aim to be as perfect as He is in this matter of giving (Matthew 5:43-6:4)

Paul's manipulative statements in this specific example fall far short of Christ's teaching, in which the widow who gave so little was commended more than other worshippers (Luke 21:1-4). Jesus had also taught that we should give from pure hearts without an expectation of earthly returns or a desire for public recognition of our acts of charity (Matthew 5:42, 6:1-4, Luke 6:35-36). While pursuing the noble objective of helping the brethren in Jerusalem, then, Paul used a wrong approach and may have ended up hurting the brethren in other churches, in addition to giving fodder to the many false apostles who have happily used his words to seek money from their own followers ever since.

It is simplistic for anyone to think that scripture teaches that the more one gives, the more they will receive from God. Quite often, in fact, the reverse could happen: Followers of Jesus are told to anticipate persecution, which may include the loss of their property (Matthew 5:11-12, Hebrews 10:32-34). The only reward we can be sure of is a rich spiritual reward, not increased material possessions.

In this matter of giving, as in the case of slavery and several other instances, the Christian must use wisdom and simply ignore the early apostles' teachings so as to pursue the royal law of love more vigorously than Paul and his contemporaries seemed ready to do.

Chapter 3

The nature and character of God

From the outset, it must be reiterated that knowledge of the full nature and character of God is beyond human comprehension. The Being that we call God, and the attributes and parameters we accord Him, are given expression in human language for the sake of our own understanding and appreciation of this Supreme Being. The manner in which God reveals Himself to anyone at some point in history does not necessarily therefore give the fullest knowledge of Him, but God designs His communication in such a way as to ensure that He reveals Himself at the person's level of understanding and cultural situation. If that were not so, it would be impossible for anyone to come to any understanding of an infinite God.

Our understanding of the nature and character of God profoundly influences our own moral values and views about the church and personal relationships. Indeed, many doctrinal conflicts can be traced to differing understandings of the nature and character of God. It is therefore crucial to have an accurate grasp of this matter if we are to become God's image on earth, thus living out truthfully as His people and church.

Current understandings of the nature and character of God

There are certain dominant strands in the understanding of the nature and character of God among believers, but with important differences. Believers are agreed that God is Almighty, omnipresent, loving, and without beginning or end.

Beyond these basics, however, disagreements emerge. While a vast majority of Christians believe that God is a Trinity of three Persons, there is a growing minority that does not hold this to be true. For those who believe in the Trinity, a majority of them are taught that the Father, Son and Holy Spirit exist in a hierarchical relationship, but a minority again hold that these three are equal.

Some Christians believe that there is a dual God-head of the Father and the Son rather than a Trinity. Some of these state that Jesus is not God, while others accord Him varying degrees of deity and power.

There are also those who uphold a Unitarian perspective; among these, there are those who claim that Jesus is not God, while others hold the view that Jesus is the same as the Father and the Holy Spirit. All sorts of beliefs and shades of opinion fall in between.

Moreover, the understanding of God's character does for most believers portray a mixture of Old Testament and New Testament beliefs. Thus, they will claim to love God while still fearing Him and not see this as a contradiction. While saying God is love, they will still attribute to Him all sorts of ugly disasters, hence the term "act of God" to refer to terrible unexpected occurrences.

The Trinity: Is God a Multiple Entity?

The teaching that God is a multiple entity of three Persons in one God-head has persisted since the days of the Church Fathers. According to this view, the Father, the Son and the Holy Spirit are three distinct Persons—each of them fully God but all three making up one and not three Gods—in what is said to be a mystery beyond human explanation.

Not all the Church Fathers believed in the trinity doctrine. Irenaeus, who lived in the second century, is reported to have said, "The Father is the invisible of the Son, but the Son is the visible of the Father" (*Against Heresies* 4.6.6, as quoted in Jonathan Hill's *The History of Christian Thought*, page 28). His other thoughts were speculative and even unscriptural, but he appears to have worked out this basic relationship between Father and Son.

Tertullian, who also lived in the second century, was the first person to use the term "trinity." He was also the first to describe the three members of this Trinity as "persons" and to talk of their unity of "substance" (*The History of Christian Thought*, page 37). He however thought of the Father as the origin of the Son and the Holy Spirit, hence having a higher stature.

Later Church Fathers continued with their guessing game, with various groups fine-tuning their fantasies on this Trinity and ascribing to it certain attributes as time went by. Others, such as the Arians, rejected the trinity and also denied the deity of Christ.

Augustine's formulation of the doctrine of the Trinity finally won the day and is what has largely persisted to this day. He agrees that the Son is the Son of the Father alone, but says that the Spirit does not only proceed from the Father, but from both the Father and the Son. He also says that the Father is not the source of divinity, and that all three Persons share in the divine nature (*The History of Christian Thought*, page 87).

We will begin our short study of this teaching of the Trinity by considering whether the Holy Spirit is indeed God.

The Holy Spirit: A Divine Being?

In all the instances where the Spirit of God is mentioned in the Old Testament, it is assumed—and this is how the prophets and their hearers must have understood it—that the Spirit is not different from God. That is how the listeners of Jesus must have understood Him, too, since they had no theology of a Spirit separate from God.

On many occasions, the "spirit" simply signifies the presence or power of God. In many instances, capitalization and the use of personal pronouns simply signifies the theological bias of translators and not linguistic accuracy. This is because many European languages assign gender to all nouns, yet in translating to English it would be nonsensical to call a book "him" rather than "it", for instance. The spirit, then, ought to have been translated as "it" on many occasions where the translations read "he."

Even where the Spirit is actually personified in the context, this should best be understood as figurative in much the same way that wisdom is personified in Proverbs 8 and 9. And just as the personification of wisdom does not lead to the conclusion that there was a person of the God-head called "Wisdom" who participated in the work of creation, so the personification of the Spirit does not make this a separate being from God. And even if it can be argued that the usage in some cases shows the Holy Spirit to be a being, this would not be a being separate from God the Father.

The spirit of a person is not a separate entity from the person. Moreover, since we know that "God is Spirit" (John 4:24), it would be nonsensical to talk of the Spirit of God as a separate entity from God, since this would then force us to also have the "Spirit of the Holy Spirit" as distinct from that Holy Spirit who is the Spirit of God. In other words, the Holy Spirit is simply the Spirit who is holy, which is a reference to God and not some other separate entity.

In the letters, the apostles did not treat the Holy Spirit as a separate entity. In their salutations and references to God, it is evident that they only acknowledged God the Father and the Lord Jesus Christ:

> Grace and peace to you from God our Father and from the Lord Jesus Christ. (Romans 1:7b)

> Grace and peace to you from God our Father and the Lord Jesus Christ, who gave himself for our sins to rescue us from the present evil age, according to the will of our God and Father, to whom be glory for ever and ever. (Galatians 1:3-5)

This acknowledgement of the Father and the Son is to be found throughout the epistles, raising the question why the apostles would be so irreverent of the Holy Spirit, if indeed there is any such being who is God separate from the Father.

Even where Paul mentions the Holy Spirit alongside the Father and the Son, it has to do with "the fellowship of the Holy Spirit" among God's people (2 Corinthians 13:14). This has to do with the spirit in which fellowship should be upheld, like praying for "the fellowship of love" in a community. It does not make the holy spirit in such cases a person.

It is striking that in the book of Revelation, John saw in his vision the throne of God and that of the Lamb (Revelation 22:3).

The "Lord God Almighty and the Lamb" are mentioned as the temple of the city of the New Jerusalem (21:22), and they also give light to the city in the next verse. Why would the Holy Spirit be left out of all these matters, even being deprived of a throne, if indeed there is any such being? The truth of scripture appears to suggest otherwise.

If ever there was such a thing as the Holy Spirit as a "Person" of God, Jesus showed that He was either not aware of such a being, or that this Holy Spirit was inexplicably kept in the dark by the other two "Persons" in this supposed Trinity:

> "All things have been committed to me by my Father. No one knows the Son except the Father, and no one knows the Father except the Son and those to whom the Son chooses to reveal him." (Matthew 11:27)

> "But about that day or hour no one knows, not even the angels in heaven, nor the Son, but only the Father." (Matthew 24:36)

Moreover, since Jesus was conceived by the power of the Holy Spirit, who would then logically be His father, the issue arises why God the Father is acknowledged in scripture as His Father rather than the Holy Spirit, if at all the two are different "Persons."

In their attempts to force the doctrine of the Trinity upon the church, the early Church Fathers—many of whom apparently never quit their pagan thinking—did not have any moral scruples with altering the biblical text. While debate on the accuracy of certain verses is inconclusive, it is quite probable that they changed Matthew 28:19 to accord with their beliefs and appear to have Jesus giving an instruction for baptism using a Trinitarian formula.

It is obvious from the Acts of the Apostles that no such Trinitarian baptismal formula was ever employed by the apostles. In fact, recent scholarship shows that it is doubtful that Jesus ever gave any instruction to baptize followers. Eusebius quotes from an early book of Matthew in his possession in his library in Caesarea. He says Jesus' actual words to his disciples in the original text of Matthew 28:19 were:

> With one word and voice He said to His disciples: "Go, and make disciples of all nations in My Name, teaching them to observe all things whatsoever I have commanded you." (*The Demonstratio Evangelica*, page 152).

Fortunately for the truth, the alterations to the bible were not done systematically enough to hide discrepancies, although these do often create confusion in the minds of believers who do not dig into the historical facts.

What is clear, however, is that the doctrine of the Trinity is a Catholic forgery by the early Church Fathers. The implications of this finding are immense. First, the Holy Spirit, without a doubt, is not God separate from the Father. This means that all the hundreds of millions of Christians who have through the ages been made to believe in the Trinity have been mixing worship of the true God with worship of something that does not exist and is not God, thus engaging in idolatry. They have been deceived into sharing their worship between God and another creature that has been prepared for them, a non-existent being whom they have equated with God—an idol.

Second, Christians have been deceived into thinking that God gave scripture that is full of mystery and cannot easily be understood through simple reasoning, thus lowering their guard and opening the door to floodgates of deception.

The end result is that although Christians claim to know God, a majority of them are really far from the knowledge of God. And if they do not know Him, how can they possibly be His image on earth? They can only provide the reflection of another god, confusing him for the true God. That is the master plan of Satan.

Having conclusively shown that there should be no worship of the Holy Spirit as a separate entity from God the Father, and that the Trinity is mere fantasy, we have to contend with whether it is then appropriate to worship the two remaining "Persons", or how to deal with each of these. As usual, it is appropriate to begin with what Jesus and the apostles said.

Jesus, the Son of God

Jesus said He was the Son of God. He said that He and the Father were one, but also acknowledged that the Father was greater than Him. Differing perspectives have been put forward over the centuries regarding these claims. While some have said that these claims of Jesus show His divinity, especially as put in the Gospel of John, others have dismissed those claims.

It is quite appropriate, therefore, to study what the apostles thought of Jesus. What was the apostles' view of Jesus and what He had said regarding Himself? How did they understand Him, and how did they conduct their own worship and prayers in light of the Jesus events?

A close scrutiny of the scriptures shows that the apostles used the term "God" to refer to the Father, while Jesus was known as "Lord" and acknowledged to be the Son of God. This pattern is evident in the salutations at the beginning of the epistles, for instance:

> Grace and peace to you from God our Father and the Lord Jesus Christ. (1 Corinthians 1:3)

> In the past God spoke to our ancestors through the prophets at many times and in various ways, but in these last days he has spoken to us by his Son, whom he appointed

heir of all things, and through whom he also made the universe. (Hebrews 1:1)

Grace and peace be yours in abundance through the knowledge of God and of Jesus our Lord. (2 Peter 1:2)

The apostles evidently held Jesus in very high esteem. In their prayers and communication, however, they addressed God the Father, while still acknowledging the role of Jesus in God's plan of redemption. They did not however equate the two, with prayers, praise and glory mainly directed at God (meaning the Father). The following examples show this pattern (emphases are mine):

Praise be **to the God and Father** of our Lord Jesus Christ, who has blessed us in the heavenly realms with every spiritual blessing in Christ... (Ephesians 1:3ff)

I keep asking that **the God of our Lord Jesus Christ, the glorious Father**, may give you the Spirit of wisdom and revelation, so that you may know him better... (Ephesians 1:17ff)

I **thank my God** every time I remember you... And this is my prayer: that your love may abound more and more in knowledge and depth of insight, so that you may be able to discern what is best and may be pure and blameless for the day of Christ, filled with the fruit of righteousness that comes through Jesus Christ—**to the glory and praise of God**. (Philippians 1:3-11)

We always **thank God, the Father of our Lord Jesus Christ**, when we pray for you, because we have heard of your faith in Christ Jesus and of the love you have for all his people... (Colossians 1:3-4)

Through Jesus, therefore, let us continually **offer to God** a sacrifice of praise—the fruit of lips that openly confess his name. (Hebrews 13:15)

> Through him **you believe in God**, who raised him from the dead and glorified him, and so **your faith and hope are in God**. (1 Peter 1:21)

This does not mean that the Son was not glorified, but this was always with reference to the Father, as these examples show (emphases are mine):

> Now may **the God of peace**, who through the blood of the eternal covenant brought back from the dead our Lord Jesus, that great Shepherd of the sheep, equip you with everything for doing his will, and may he work in us what is pleasing to him, through Jesus Christ, to whom be glory for ever and ever. Amen. (Hebrews 13:20-21)

> To him who loves us and has freed us from our sins by his blood, and has made us to be a kingdom and priests **to serve his God and Father**—to him be glory and power for ever and ever! Amen. (Revelation 1:5b-6)

It would appear that the apostles were careful to maintain a distinction between their love and respect for Jesus as their Lord, the head of the church and ruler of God's creation, on the one hand, and recognition of God the Father as God, on the other. When Paul enumerated the essential points of Christian unity to the Ephesians, among the seven items mentioned were "one Lord" and "one God and Father of all" (Ephesians 4:4-6). He did not use terminology such as "one God in two Persons" or "one God in three Persons." Obviously, to the early church, "Lord" and "God" were not synonymous.

Even though John ascribes praise, honour and glory to both God the Father and Jesus in the book of Revelation, he is careful to maintain this distinction. In Revelation 4 and 5, the one who sits on the throne is God, while the Lamb, who "took the scroll from the right hand of him who sat on the throne," (Revelation 5:7) is obviously Jesus.

In Revelation 22, the last chapter of the bible, both God and the Lamb are seen seated on thrones. The Lamb, however, is not called God, and the distinction between the two is clearly maintained.

Does this mean that the apostles did not believe in the divinity of Jesus? While they were careful not to call Jesus "God" directly, from their writings one can see that they actually attributed to Jesus certain activities and attributes that are specific to God. The following are examples of this:

1. In Philippians 2:6, Paul says that Christ Jesus was "in very nature God" and had "equality with God" before He decided to take on human likeness. The writer to the Hebrews makes a statement that also puts Christ at the level of God, saying "The Son is the radiance of God's glory and the exact representation of his being." Since according to the Old Testament scriptures God has no equal and nobody can measure up to Him, these statements can only mean that these two writers were claiming that Jesus is God.

2. While Genesis 1:1 tells us in no uncertain terms that "God created the heavens and the earth," Paul ascribes this role to Jesus in Colossians 1:16, thus indirectly telling us that Jesus is the God of the Old Testament. The writer to the Hebrews agrees with him, saying that Jesus "made the universe" (Hebrews 1:2).

3. Peter says that Jesus spoke through the prophets of the

Old Testament:

> Concerning this salvation, the prophets, who spoke of the grace that was to come to you, searched intently and with the greatest care, trying to find out the time and circumstances to which the Spirit of Christ in them was pointing when he predicted the sufferings of Christ and the glories that would follow. (1 Peter 1:10-11)

> Yet, we know from the Old Testament that the prophets were given the messages they spoke by God, which would mean by inference that Peter is here saying that the God who spoke to the prophets was Jesus, and the Spirit of Christ he mentions is therefore what the Old Testament calls the Spirit of God.

4. John records Jesus as telling him that He is "the First and the Last" (Revelation 1:17), and again, "I am the Alpha and the Omega, the First and the Last, the Beginning and the End" (Revelation 22:13). These phrases echo the words of the prophets when speaking of the Almighty God, as in Isaiah: "I am the First and the Last; apart from me there is no God" (Isaiah 44:6). The import of these words could not have been lost on people who were well-versed in the Old Testament—that John was essentially saying that Jesus declares He is God.

It would appear, then, that while the apostles understood Jesus to be God, they did not openly acknowledge Him as such. This could partly have been due to their Jewish background, as it would have been difficult to evangelize the Jews while telling them that a man who was in their midst just a few years earlier had been the face of the Almighty God. The demands of the day may well have forced them to opt for terminology that was easier for their hearers, while retaining the core of their teaching about Jesus buried deep in their testimonies and epistles.

It seems that the word "Lord" served this purpose well and did not mean to the apostles the same thing as the word "God". In many languages, the two words may be used inter-changeably, blurring the line between God the Father and Jesus. The apostles did not seem to have had any such struggle, and while they spoke of Jesus in flowery terms, their prayers and worship were directed primarily at God the Father.

Taking the context of the whole of scripture into account, what then does the Bible teach us about God, and about Jesus in relation to God? Were the apostles right in directing their worship primarily to God (the Father) while still treating Jesus very highly yet obviously a rung lower than the Father? Should we understand this to have been a concession to Judaism, as intimated earlier? In that case, should we therefore ignore their example—as most of Christendom has done today—and declare Jesus is not just Lord but God too? Is there a point at which the apostles erred in this matter, as they did in others?

Whatever the result of any investigation into this matter, it is obvious that any Christian or church that wants to strictly maintain the practice of the early apostles would have to not only discard worship of the Holy Spirit as a separate "Person" of God, but also to treat Jesus only as Lord in open discourse while acknowledging that He is God in a less straightforward manner and remaining ambivalent about the relationship between Him and the Father.

That also means focusing all public worship on the Father, as our God, even as we exalt the name of Jesus as Lord. That was the pattern established by the apostles. Whatever explanations may be offered about the place of Jesus as God in Christian worship, however, the biblical fact is that the apostles never set forth any pattern for a multiplicity of "Persons" who would all be worshipped as God.

Anyone who stops at this stage as set by the apostles would have arrived at the stage of restoration of biblical truth. But because the apostles were often wrong or did not go far enough, restoration is not the aim of this book. We must retrace our footsteps to see the truths the first church had arrived at, and then move beyond these to reach the state of perfection that God desires.

Can we therefore interrogate this matter further, while remaining thoroughly biblical, and see what other conclusions are possible, or in what manner the apostles may have failed to gain a deeper understanding of the topic? Is it possible to go beyond the conceptualization of the early apostles while retaining the apostolic spirit?

Jesus was God among us—in other words, a manifestation of God Himself. It would therefore be worth looking at the history of how God has manifested Himself to man in scripture in order to unravel the mystery of Jesus' identity and His relationship with God the Father.

Physical manifestations of God

In His efforts to reach out to man, God has often gone out of His way to reveal Himself in unexpected ways. Apart from dreams and visions, inner promptings and even audible voice, God has sometimes revealed Himself in physical form. A few examples will elucidate this point.

(i)   We are told that Adam and Eve "heard the sound of the Lord God as he was walking in the garden in the cool of the day, and they hid from the Lord God (Genesis 3:8). After God called them out, He proceeded to speak to them and tell them the consequences of their disobedience. The physical manifestation of God in this instance should not make us think that there is a second "Person" of God, and neither does the bible make any such claims.

(ii)   Genesis 18 recounts God's meeting with Abraham "near the great trees of Mamre." Before the three visitors left, God told Abraham that his wife Sarah would give birth by about the same time in the following year. God then revealed to Abraham his plans to destroy Sodom, and Abraham started pleading for that city.

Whatever profound effect this meeting with God must have had on Abraham, it did not make him begin a theology of a Person of God who is a man and another Person of God in heaven. He seems to have understood that God had simply manifested Himself in human form to converse with him, but remained the one mighty God who controls the heavens and earth.

(iii)   In the account of Moses and the burning bush (Exodus 3), God in His wisdom raised Moses' curiosity through a bush that burnt but was not consumed, then spoke to him from within the bush. But He remained the same One God and there was no intention of creating a new "God of the Burning Bush."

(iv)   The second chapter of Judges records that the angel of the Lord went up from Gilgal to Bokim and spoke to the people, reminding them of how He had rescued them from Egypt and how they had broken His covenant with them. The Israelites, once again, understood that God had simply taken upon Himself the form of an angel. They did not try to create a teaching of a second Person of God who is an angel.

(v)   In chapter six of the book of Judges, the angel of God this time appears to Gideon, sending him to fight against the Midianites. He even allowed Gideon to test him, gladly offering the miraculous signs that would have convinced Gideon that indeed it was the Lord who was sending him. Once again, however, no theology that separates the earthly manifestation of God from the eternal God came about—in his own way, Gideon perfectly understood that the angel of God who had appeared to him was only a manifestation of God and not a separate Person.

(vi)   The birth of Samson (Judges 13) is yet another instance when the Lord manifested Himself in angelic form. The bible records that the angel of the Lord appeared first to Manoah's wife, and then returned on a second occasion in response to Manoah's prayer. Even this time, the Israelites were sufficiently knowledgeable not to create a theology of a second Person of God, despite multiple appearances of God in human and angelic form in the course their history.

Since God is almighty, He is able to talk to multiple people on earth in varied ways at the same time—whether through audible voice, dreams and visions, or physical appearances. That truth does not validate any theology of a multiple personhood.

Many Trinitarian bible scholars claim that the appearances of God recorded in the Old Testament were actually those of the second Person of the Godhead, Jesus Christ, and that the Father does not appear to men in physical form. But this reasoning is nowhere found in scripture. The bible simply records that God has appeared in the many instances mentioned. It does not state that the angel of the Lord was different from Jehovah, the Father. The only conclusion we can deduce is that God appeared to men time and again in human or angelic form, before finally manifesting himself through being born and dwelling in their midst for 30 or so years.

Yes, it was Jesus, as the Everlasting Father and Most High God in Isaiah's writings, who appeared to men, but He is one God and not a "Second Person" following another higher Person of God. To make such a claim – that there is anyone above Him – is to deny Him all the glory that He deserves.

In addition to the above examples, we find that God is referred to in multiple ways in the Old Testament, but with the understanding by all worshippers that this was indeed the same God. In the very first verse of Genesis, he is "God", while in the second verse we are told that the "Spirit of God" was hovering over the waters. Throughout the Old Testament, the terms "Spirit of God" or "Spirit of the Lord" could as well be replaced with simply "God" to the same effect. Depending on the manner in which He reveals Himself, He is also given other terms by men, such as "Adonai" and "Jireh," but that does not make Him more than one Person.

A manifestation comes and goes, but God remains forever. Moses was attracted to the burning bush, and this was God's way of revealing Himself to Moses. When Moses listened to the voice emanating from the burning bush, He was listening to God. The burning bush, through which God spoke and sent Moses to deliver the Israelites from bondage, did not receive glory, it being understood that it is God who was speaking through the burning bush; only He should therefore get the glory.

Later, God manifested Himself as a human being, and those who listen to the voice of Jesus and obey Him glorify the same God. The kind of manifestations may differ, but the purpose remains to fulfil God's plan and bring glory to Him. The manifestation is not a being separate from God to receive glory that is divorced from glory to God. This consideration may have influenced the apostles in their prayers and epistles, because we see them directing their attention primarily to the Father and only secondarily to Jesus.

As discussed earlier, this was also perhaps due to the Jewish situation, whereby it would have been difficult for people to understand that Jesus was actually God manifested in the flesh. With a proper understanding, however, we know today that we can pray to, give glory and honour to Jesus so long as we acknowledge that He is the same God and not a different "Person."

In the Old Testament, after initially introducing the manifestation in the various instances, the text then makes it clear that it is God who is speaking. The words spoken are not necessarily attributed to "the burning bush" or "angel of the Lord," but God Himself. Thus, we are told that God spoke to Moses, and not that the burning bush spoke to him. Even where the angel of the Lord is given the credit, it is eventually made clear that this was really God speaking.

The same is true of Jesus. When we take a statement such as, "Jesus commanded us to love one another," we can as well replace "Jesus" with "God" to the same effect. The earthly, historical Jesus was as much a temporary manifestation of the Almighty God as the burning bush and the angelic appearances were. This means that there was no pre-existent "Son of God" in heaven before the Lord's incarnation, just as there was no pre-existent burning bush. Various texts in the Old Testament make it abundantly clear that God was alone and without any helper:

"I am the Lord,

who has made all things,

who alone stretched out the heavens,

who spread out the earth by myself." (Isaiah 44:24b)

The New Testament, of course, says Jesus created all things (John 1:3, Hebrews 1:2). This is not a contradiction, given that Jesus was simply a manifestation of God. His name may therefore be used synonymously with God, but with the understanding that we would then be referring to God in His everlasting form and not the temporary manifestation. A Trinitarian position would however result in a contradiction that makes God a liar in verses such as the one above, since He would be claiming He wasn't helped whereas Jesus helped Him out, if indeed Jesus is different from the Father.

It is worthwhile to remember that God is spirit (John 4:24), and nobody should think that there is any part of God that is not spirit. God is not a material being. When we claim that Jesus and the Father are persons separate from the Holy Spirit, we insinuate that a part of God is not spirit, or that there are three different Spirits of God.

Far from what many Christians take for granted, the New Testament nowhere teaches that the Father, Son and Holy Spirit are three "Persons" of the one God. That is a teaching that came from attempts by the Church Fathers to make sense of statements by Jesus and the apostles mentioning God, the Father, the Son, the Holy Spirit, the Spirit of God, the Spirit of Christ, and so forth. But we know that the Church Fathers were human and made many mistakes, some of which afflict the church to this day. We are under no obligation to follow their lead blindly, but must seek to pursue the truth of scripture to its logical conclusion.

In the same way that the use of different terms to refer to God in the Old Testament did not denote different "Persons" of God, there is no evidence in the New Testament that this situation has changed.

The teaching of Jesus

Jesus Christ came to reveal God. He said He had come from God and that He was the Son of God. The word "Son" could only have been used for our own benefit and ease of understanding, since God cannot evidently have children in the human sense of the word. It could only have meant, then, one who is a representation of the Father. God is spirit and is everywhere, but here was someone who had come in the likeness of man, yet He was God.

Unlike previous instances in the Old Testament when God appeared in human or angelic form to people for short periods of time, this time He came to live in their midst so as to reveal Himself to them more fully. But the duration of stay, or the manner of His coming (by birth through a woman rather than previous sudden appearances and disappearances) did not diminish the fact that this was God in all His fullness taking on the form of a human being. It did not, either, make the specific form in which He appeared, in this case Jesus Christ, to become a separate Person of God, just as previous appearances were not deemed that way. God, for whom nothing is impossible, continued to be Spirit and to be present everywhere even as He at His own choosing revealed Himself as a human or angelic being limited in space and time, all the while remaining one and the same God.

As previously mentioned, God comes down to speak to people at the level of their understanding. He also speaks in parables and figures of speech that ought to be understood only within the context in which they are used. Jesus' words were "full of the Spirit and life" (John 6:63) and any interpretation that treats His words at a worldly level of understanding would obviously miss the point.

When Jesus speaks of "Father" and "Son," this cannot be taken as proof that these are two different persons in the same way that a human father and son would be two persons. The most logical reasoning, in the light of previous physical appearances of God, would be that the "Son" is a reference to the physical manifestation of God limited in space and time, while the "Father" refers to the spiritual aspect—the God of all eternity who remains spirit and controls all things.

When the angel Gabriel visited Mary to tell her about the pregnancy she was about to carry, he told her that the child she will conceive "will be called the Son of God" (Luke 1:35). This tells us that the term "Son of God" is a reference to the earthly Jesus.

This reasoning also agrees with Paul's words to the Colossians that "the Son is the image of the invisible God" (Colossians 1:15). Conversely, then, the Father would obviously be the invisible of the Son. The Father-Son relationship has nothing to do with birth, age, seniority, or any other issues arising from human cultural relationships.

But has the Son of God always existed? If the Son of God is merely the image of God, or to put it more clearly a temporary manifestation of the Father, then it follows that it is not possible that there was such a thing as a Son of God before the conception of Jesus—even going by the angel Gabriel's words to Mary. In the same way that there was no pre-existent burning bush before God appeared to Moses in a bush, there could not have been a pre-existent Son of God before God took on human form. But God has always existed and will continue to do so, outliving every manifestation He may take. The pre-existent Christ that the apostles refer to in some of their writings, of course, was no less than God Himself, who remains one and has no multiplicity in His Being.

Moreover, just as after the temporary manifestations of the burning bush and angel of the Lord left they did not continue to exist as entities in heaven separate from God, the heavenly Jesus is similarly not an entity in heaven separate from the Father. But being a God who comes down to our level of comprehension, He spoke to Paul as Jesus, and later did the same to John in the book of Revelation—thus planting the impression that the Lord is different from the Father. But we who have the whole scripture would do well to put all these issues into perspective, declaring that Jesus is the Father and the Spirit.

God came to live among us in human form, referred to by a name like the rest of us (Jesus), eating and drinking in our midst. The purpose was to lovingly draw us back to God. This means that God, who is spirit, remained the same one God he had always been, but there was now a physical manifestation of this God in human form for our sake. But this does not in any way mean that there were now two "Persons" of God. When the temporary manifestation left the world, the eternal God continued reigning, as usual, as one God.

Since it was God who caused His own temporary manifestation to appear in a physical form as Jesus Christ of Nazareth, we can rightly say that Jesus was begotten of God. Human beings, although created by God, are begotten by their parents. This is why the bible says that Adam begat Seth, and Seth begat Enos. Jesus did not have human parents, and we can only say He was begotten of God.

Because He was begotten, it means the earthly Jesus had a beginning. This is only logical and should not be surprising: The burning bush had a beginning and an end, and every human as well as angelic manifestation of God can be said to have had a beginning point and an ending. That does not mean God had a beginning or has an end, but only in His physical manifestations. And because Jesus is God, in that eternal form He has neither beginning nor end.

The earthly Jesus, then, or the Son of God for that matter, was created and begotten, having had a beginning when He was conceived and an end when He ascended into heaven. The Son was created, but God is not; the Son was begotten, but God is not.

The Son of God, which essentially is an expression meaning the visible image of the invisible God, not only had a beginning but also an end. God is spirit, and the fact that Jesus ascended into heaven should not make anyone imagine that He retains a human body in heaven. It is just as when God disappeared from view in His previous appearances, this did not mean that those physical forms continued living in heaven. Since there is no visible image of God in heaven, there is no Son of God who exists beyond the ascension of Jesus into heaven. Jesus is God and no longer the Son of God.

Trinitarians sometimes use the term "God the Son," which would refer to Jesus as a permanent Son throughout eternity in relation to God the Father. However, this term is nowhere used in the bible. Scripture recognizes the Son of God, but no such figure as a God the Son who dwells in eternal sonship. It is a concept that should not be entertained by anybody who takes the bible seriously. There is simply no such being as God the Son.

The fact that there is a Son of God does not mean there must necessarily be a Mother of God, or a Brother of God, or any such relationship. Since scripture repeatedly mentions God the Father, that is no reason to come up with a theology of God the Son, or God the Mother, or God the Brother. Such relationships are created by carnal minds intent on following their own speculative misadventures—a shameful preoccupation in which Augustine excelled, in the process imprisoning millions of minds over the centuries.

If God is spirit, will He once again manifest Himself in a physical form? That is entirely at His discretion. In fact, the bible records that at the second coming, "Every eye will see him, even those who pierced him" (Revelation 1:7). It is not some human form of God kept in heaven that will come down, but God will manifest Himself once again in a visible form—which is what scripture calls the Son of God.

Had Jesus come declaring immediately and directly that He was a physical manifestation of Almighty God in our midst, what would have been the consequences? He had not come for a short-term task after which He would disappear into thin air, as was the case in the Old Testament theophanies, or appearances of God in physical form. He was here to stay in our midst, as one of us, and wanted to communicate the things of God at the level of understanding of the community He had chosen to be born into. To gain real understanding at a higher level, we must seek to know what issues He simplified, how and why He did that, and what the proper understanding should be.

Because scripture says that at the baptism of Jesus, "the Holy Spirit descended on him in bodily form like a dove" (Luke 3:21), we would be foolish to begin teaching that the Holy Spirit has the physical form of a dove. Neither should we teach that this Holy Spirit is a separate "Person" of God or different from the Spirit of God mentioned in Isaiah and the Prophets. Simplification, figures of speech, parables and other literary devices are intended to bring about ease of understanding, not extraction of unintended meanings.

Since Christ simplified many matters to a level that the people would understand Him, we must have the overall view of scripture to get His meaning clearly and avoid meanings not intended by the context. For instance, He said He will ask the Father to send the Spirit of truth, the Advocate, to be with His disciples and to teach them all truth. But who is the Spirit of truth if not God Himself? And isn't it clear from the epistles that this was also the Spirit of Christ (Romans 8:9)? And because the Lord is the Spirit (2 Corinthians 3:17-18), it is as if Jesus was saying, "I will no longer be with you in this temporary physical manifestation of God in which you have known me, but will be with you as God, in spirit." That kind of statement, deciphered in this manner, does not turn God into several persons, but leaves Him as one God.

That Jesus was not teaching about God being some sort of committee of different entities can be discerned from His own words, in which He asserts that He and the Father are one. He did not say that they were two different "Persons," with the Holy Spirit a third one, and men have no right to formulate what He never said. Sample these verses:

> I and the Father are one. (John 10:30)

> Do not believe me unless I do the works of my Father. But if I do them, even though you do not believe me, believe the works, that you may know and understand that the Father is in me, and I in the Father. (John 10:37-38)

> If you really know me, you will know my Father as well. From now on, you do know him and have seen him... Anyone who has seen me has seen the Father. How can you say, 'Show us the Father'? Don't you believe that I am in the Father, and that the Father is in me? The words I say to you I do not speak on my own authority. Rather, it is the Father, living in me, who is doing his work. Believe me when I say that I am in the Father and the Father is in me; or at least believe on the evidence of the works themselves. (John 14:7-11)

Apostolic understanding of the Father-Son relationship

As was explained in previous chapters, the apostles gained a greater understanding after the departure of Christ and outpouring of the Spirit than had been gained during His stay with them, but still this was by no means complete.

The apostles spoke of God mainly with reference to the Father. They also wrote about the Son, and the Spirit with respect to both the Father and the Son. But there were no firm boundaries. In Paul's epistles, in fact, he easily interchanges references such as God, the Father, Son, Christ, and Spirit. The following examples are pertinent:

(i) In Acts 20:28, Paul exhorts the Ephesian elders to "keep watch over yourselves and all the flock of which the Holy Spirit has made you overseers." Yet, in Ephesians 4:11, Paul says it is Christ who gave the church apostles, prophets, evangelists, pastors and teachers (hence the overseers mentioned in Acts 20:28).

(ii) Paul mentions to the Corinthians that the Lord (Jesus Christ) is the Spirit: "Now the Lord is the Spirit, and where the Spirit of the Lord is, there is freedom. And we all, who with unveiled faces contemplate the Lord's glory, are being transformed into his image with ever-increasing glory, which comes from the Lord, who is the Spirit" (2 Corinthians 3: 17-18).

(iii) In Acts 15:11, Peter tells the assembly in Jerusalem that "it is through the grace of the Lord Jesus that we are saved." In Ephesians 2:6-8, however, Paul suggests that this grace is from the Father, declaring "it is the gift of God" (both the context and the term "God" show that Paul is referring to the Father). Words such as "grace" and "mercy" are freely ascribed to both Father and Son throughout the New Testament.

Having been profoundly influenced by Christ during His stay with them, it is only natural that the apostles would see everything through that prism—with a heavy dose of Jewish thinking—and fail to see the big picture. They therefore spoke of how the Lord Jesus had come down from heaven and, after His death and resurrection, ascended to sit on the right hand of the Father. They did not see that God had come down in human manifestation and then left, remaining God just as He was before.

If it is indeed true that Christ is God, then He must have been God even before coming down to earth. That is why He says, "Before Abraham was born, I am" (John 8:58). The apostles also recognize this, with Paul saying that the spiritual rock that the Israelites drank from in the wilderness was Christ (1 Corinthians 10:3-4). If Christ already had this exalted position well before coming down to live among us, having even created the heavens and the earth, how then would it at all be possible to gain a promotion to another "highest place" with "a name that is above every name" (Philippians 2:9)? No, there can be no promotion above being God, which He already was—He must simply have continued with the glory that He has always had as God Most High.

This doxology by Paul in Philippians and similar ones by the apostles, therefore, cannot be taken as teaching about an elevated place for Christ after his ascension into heaven, separate from the seat of God. The apostles were simply elated, as anyone would be given the joy of salvation, and were ecstatically expressing that joy regardless of whether what they were stating was doctrinally correct or not.

Jesus had talked numerous times about His Father, but like with other weaknesses of the apostles, they did not pause to ponder the meaning of those words. They went about talking and writing about Jesus and the Father without thinking much over the issues involved – or if they did, found it expedient within their context to underplay the truth about the full deity of Christ.

Because of the huge impact the earthly Jesus had left among them, when God spoke to the apostles, He revealed Himself to them as Jesus. We know "Jesus" is an earthly name like any other, which God in His physical manifestation on earth was known by—it is not a heavenly name and God has no name, really. If God wants to speak to somebody who understands the Kiswahili language and knows God as "Mungu," He will reveal Himself as "Mungu." God continued, therefore, revealing Himself to the apostles and others in the manner they would most easily have understood Him as, "Jesus."

Indeed, in the book of Revelation, Jesus still reveals Himself as a man (Revelation 1:13). It is not because He has taken human form in heaven, since God is spirit, but this was a vision given simply for John's (and our own) understanding.

In the same manner, John is given a vision of a beautiful city, the New Jerusalem, which is the city of God; but we know the city we expect to inherit is a heavenly one, which no eye has seen and no ear heard and whose beauty is indescribable in human terms. This means that God was simply giving a preview of the beauty that believers should expect in the after-life using human terms of John's time, so as to encourage this apostle and other Christians to withstand the persecutions they were going through for the sake of their eternal inheritance. We cannot, however, use the description of the New Jerusalem to state that heaven is like that.

In the same vein, we cannot say that the throne of heaven is as John describes it (Revelation 4), or that that there is "a Lamb, looking as if it had been slain" (Revelation 5:6), or that any of the myriad creatures that John saw are actually to be found in heaven. John even wrote about God having seven spirits (Revelation 1:4) and seven stars in His right hand (Revelation 2:1), but we cannot use such verses to claim that God is a unity of seven Persons. God was simply speaking figuratively in a manner that we can comprehend, which has still proved difficult to understand given the numerous misinterpretations of scripture throughout history.

Today, when we pray "in the name of Jesus," God understands our situation and answers our prayers. It is not because of a formula of words, but because we are calling upon Him as God. He has only simplified matters for us by calling Himself "Jesus," thus coming down to a level we can relate with by having a name like one of us. He remains one God, who has always been there and lives forever, in spirit, powerful and beyond what the human mind can comprehend. There is no multiplicity in His Being.

What about the question of Jesus being "at the right hand of the Father" and other statements that appear to show that Jesus is distinct from God the Father? Some people have explained this by saying that the risen Christ could be having such a manifestation in heaven, which will last until his enemies will have been made "a footstool" for His feet (Psalm 110:1, Hebrews 1:13).

While on the face of it this presents a possibility, unfortunately there is little evidence that this is in fact the case. In heaven, Jesus Christ is spirit, and the Spirit of Christ is no different from the Spirit of God. When we read about Jesus being seated at the right hand of the Father, therefore, this could either have been for the purposes of making the gospel palatable to Jews or a display of a deficient understanding by the early apostles, for indeed Jesus is Himself the Father and is seated on the throne of God!

Since the Son of God was the visible expression of God, it means that following the ascension into heaven and the end of that physical manifestation, Jesus ceased to be the Son of God. He is no longer the Son of God but God Himself, just as He had always been for eternity past. That means those who worship a Son of God and pray to Him honour a non-existent entity, just in the same way as those who pray to the Holy Spirit as a separate being of God do. Many Christians actually dishonour Jesus by referring to him as a Son and placing Him second in their man-created hierarchy, when Jesus is actually the mighty invisible God. And by worshipping a non-existent entity that they say is second to God, they are guilty of idolatry.

No sharing of glory

God says He will not share His glory with another and forbids worship of anything else—He is a jealous God. We are then confronted with a difficult situation in Hebrews 1, which says God commanded angels to worship Jesus. If Jesus is worthy of worship, therefore, He would have to be one and the same with the Father. If not, He would at most be Lord but not God.

What exactly did Jesus mean by saying that He and the Father were one? He did not say they were two "Persons," but said they were one. That means that there can be only one indivisible God, and that Jesus was merely the manifestation of God for man's benefit. In heaven, then, there can be only one God.

Why then did John see two thrones in Revelation 22, one for God and another for the Lamb? Since God speaks according to our understanding and expectations, He showed the early church two thrones because the early church had not arrived at the full implications of the understanding that Jesus was a manifestation or visible image of the one God. The church instead taught that Jesus had been exalted to sit at the right hand of God—meaning very close to the heartbeat of God, but still not God. Insights of the truth that Jesus is God were however discernible, even if hidden, within the epistles.

To make an analogy, a believer who has been made to think that to be properly saved one must go through an ecstatic experience of tongue-speaking will be granted that gift by our loving Father. When God does that, we should not think that He is giving His approval for the theology of a second baptism of the Holy Spirit, nor that He is showing His approval for the doctrine of the Trinity. God simply overlooks our ignorance of all these matters and approves of our desire to move closer to Him by granting our wishes, so long as these are not ungodly. He even overlooks the fact that many times our desires for spiritual gifts are born out of selfish ambition and pride, because we desire to show off our "godliness" to others in the church, while remaining quite distant from Him in the measure of love toward other brethren.

To give another example, when God works in someone the desire to take a leap of faith toward salvation, He uses the understanding of that person to make Him move closer to the group of brethren or local denomination that presents the image of godliness to that person. God does not from the beginning tell the new convert about the weaknesses of that denomination and the manner in which its adherents may be deceived. His approval of the new believer's fellowship with a particular congregation cannot be argued as proof of His approval of the group's doctrines or practices.

The vision that God gave John in the book of Revelation, in which John saw a throne of God and another of the Lamb, can be understood in the same manner. In actual fact, the Lamb and God are one and the same.

Consequences for evangelism

Unitarianism makes it easy to evangelize monotheistic groups such as Jews and Muslims. Trinitarianism makes it unnecessarily difficult for such groups to accept Christ, seeing that Christianity appears to teach a multiplicity of gods.

Even for previously polytheistic converts, Trinitarianism offers no real advantage. It may be easier for believers of multi-deity pagan faiths to accept Christianity, but the impact of their new-found faith is lost. They would be moving to a faith that still has the multiplicity of gods to worship that they were previously accustomed to; their new faith becomes simply a continuation of their former beliefs and does not demand obedience to the one single, supreme God that Christianity stands for. This spirit of compromise on such a core matter is replicated elsewhere in various teachings, greatly diminishing the power of the gospel. An attitude that the gospel can be changed to accommodate the worldly interests of communities is thus cultivated.

The Character of God

Much of what has been discussed so far gives an excellent idea of the character of God, so this will be just a brief summary of this topic.

God is infinite in all positive respects: wisdom, intellect, knowledge, and every other positive attribute in its perfection. He is complete in Himself, but desires that He be glorified in His creation, principally man. When we excel in any positive achievement, we reflect God's character.

In His attitude toward mankind, God displays infinite goodness, mercy, grace, kindness, patience and long-suffering.

God is always good and can never be responsible for evil, which comes from the devil. He desires that the whole world be saved, but will not force His will on anybody. Those who accept his offer of salvation are saved, while those who reject it are condemned and end up in hell solely on their own volition.

In his dealings with man, God will normally operate organically. He will influence everyday occurrences that we take for granted, and only a regenerate spirit will recognize the Lord's doing. Of course, He will occasionally go against natural laws in a display of supernatural power, but this is not the norm. On a day-to-day basis, He works within our natural environment and situations to bring good, even painfully slowly by our own thinking.

Since God desires that our worship and obedience should flow naturally from our hearts, He will normally not flex muscles to force people to do something that He desires. For sure, He will whisper His desires quietly to everyone's heart, but will not cause an earthquake to make it happen.

Quite often, people take the attitude that if something is of God, He will make it come to pass, but only rarely is this true. This kind of reasoning is used as an excuse to refuse to do God's will and come out of that disobedience with a straight face, since after all God never came out to oppose you openly. But He continues whispering into your heart, which you can obviously simply ignore, yet the disobedience is clear deep inside you.

This means that it takes a quiet spirit to hear God's voice. Anyone who thinks that loud arguments and displays of power will bring out God's will is obviously greatly mistaken. More often than not, our God can almost be said to be shy. He is found in the silence rather than the noise, in humility rather than displays of strength, and in submission rather than conquest.

Because of man's false impression and hopes that God comes to fight our battles in a show of power, we tend to confuse earthly possessions and power with God's blessing. Scripture teaches otherwise, as can be discerned from the whole earthly life of Jesus. The lives of the prophets and apostles offer the same lesson, so it is quite ridiculous to find Christians who to this day associate temporal power and possessions with God's power and approval, and lack thereof with God's displeasure or lack of blessing. To be sure, God does not want His people to live in want or abject poverty, yet this is not the standard by which God's anointing on somebody is to be measured. If it were, people such as John the Baptist would have been very far from God, having been feeding on insects in the wilderness as the priests in the temple continued eating the delicacies of animal offerings.

God wishes that those who desire to know Him better should seek Him diligently. Partly, this is for the purpose of training us and in the process establishing a constant relationship with Him. He will therefore allow us to practically search long and hard for answers from Him before responding.

God searches the heart and is interested in inner purity. He detests hypocrisy and legalistic obedience that is devoid of love. Showmanship and anything meant to promote a selfish agenda do not please Him.

Chapter 4

The identity of true and counterfeit churches

The term "false church" is something of a misnomer, since a church that is not true is not a church at all in the first place. In the same way that counterfeit money is not money in the real sense but worthless paper designed to deceive genuine users of money in our cash economies, false churches are a counterfeit expression of church that does not bring glory to God.

There are two levels at which the word "church" is normally applied. At the first level, all believers belong to the body of Christ and are part of the same church. Since it is not practical for all believers worldwide to meet in one place for fellowship, however, the bible recognizes the faithful at each locality as constituting a church, hence the churches in Corinth, Ephesus, Antioch and other places.

It is at this second level that false churches manifest themselves. This means that a genuine believer who belongs to a false local church will still remain a member of the spiritual body of Christ, the universal church. Such a believer is therefore assured of his or her place in paradise, but will not bear much fruit for the Lord in this life by virtue of staying in the wrong spiritual environment.

It is what happens at the group or corporate level that shows whether a church is true or counterfeit. Of course, this will also have a great impact on what happens at the individual level. It is at the corporate level that teaching is done and the believer's priesthood asserted or denied, influencing the individual's belief system and walk with God. This is what Satan aims to subvert using false churches.

A true church that aims for perfection is necessarily apostolic, having its attention fixed on the heavenly Christ and at His disposal to undertake His mission in the world. A sure way of telling whether a church is walking in the true apostolic spirit or not is therefore to check how much it is focused on Christ vis-à-vis other interests that unsuspectingly creep in.

Conversely, a false church can never be apostolic. While it may claim to be Christ-centred, in actual fact it will take up structures and undertake programs and activities whose end result is to push people's focus farther away from Christ. While in theory it will preach Christ, in practice it will limit and hinder the work of God, giving only superficial obedience to Christ.

The natural environment for a believer is the true church. That is what God has ordained. Satan, in his attempts to create confusion among the brethren, plants false churches and tries to make it as difficult as possible to distinguish these from true churches. This entails making false churches take on some characteristics of true churches. It therefore takes discernment to tell the two apart, and the believer who does not exercise spiritual diligence will easily fall for the counterfeit.

This is not to say that believers should never attend the gatherings of false churches. However, this is done for specific purposes of advancing the Lord's work, much in the same way that Paul stood in the Aeropagus and spoke to people who worshipped idols, including an "unknown God" (Acts 17:19-23). The believer should never attend such meetings for the purpose of seeking genuine Christian fellowship. On a regular basis and for fellowship, the gathering of the apostolic church is where the believer will be found.

It is also important to recognize that just as there are true believers who have unfortunately been deceived to fellowship in false churches, false brethren will also occasionally turn up in true churches. The latter are planted by Satan to try and sow division and false teachings in true churches. A vigilant church under the Spirit's guidance will easily make it impossible for such brethren to operate and they soon quit and go where they belong.

While the true church is under God's headship, Satan is in control of false churches, where his servants are in charge (2 Corinthians 11:13-15). The distinguishing characteristic that determines whether a church is true or counterfeit, therefore, has to do with the power behind it. While God is almighty and His power can still be made evident among true believers in false churches, this power is greatly hindered in such counterfeit manifestations of church. Of course, every false church claims to be following the leading of the Holy Spirit, yet the distinguishing characteristics of false churches will be obvious.

This is not about whether the bible is read or not, whether the name of Jesus is proclaimed or not, or even whether the believers in such a church are truly saved or not. Paul was clear that not everyone proclaims Christ out of pure motives (Philippians 1:15-18). Even though Christ is preached in all circumstances, we need to ask ourselves: Why would anyone want to preach Christ out of impure motives?

The reason has to do with misleading believers and preventing them from fully living according to the plan of God. It is a ploy of the enemy to discourage believers and destroy their walk with God. False teachings are introduced, the priesthood of the believer is destroyed, and the believer's focus is progressively removed from Christ.

In the process, many believers have ended up destroying their walk with God, which is Satan's aim in raising false churches. To use again an example of genuine versus counterfeit money, it is obvious to the whole world that we do not reject money just because there is counterfeit money in circulation. No, we try to know the features of the genuine currency so well that we would easily identify any counterfeit money coming our way. That is how we should also handle counterfeit churches: Get to know what God says about His church so well that when Satan shows up with the counterfeit, no true believer would bother with it.

Satan will use greed for power and money to achieve his aims of creating confusion among the brethren, by which there is no shortage of false apostles to carry out his devious schemes. Scripture will be read, yes, but cleverly twisted to teach falsehoods. The name of Jesus will be proclaimed, but His power not allowed to become manifest. Believers in such churches will therefore be spiritually disarmed and rendered completely powerless.

Since the natural home of the believer is the church under the headship of Christ, true believers who are in spiritual Babylon cannot freely fulfil the purposes of God. Obviously, it is the Lord's desire that they should go back to the true, apostolic church.

Again, because believers who are in false churches are still part of the body of Christ, the brethren in true churches are bound to love them, even though they must not approve of their sectarianism.

While true churches may be deficient in knowledge and practice to a certain extent, the more they exhibit the signs of false churches, the more they stifle the Lord's operation in their midst. A really apostolic church will be open to correction and continuous purification by the word of God.

When true believers find themselves in false churches, Satan will oppress them using his messengers, whom the bible declares will masquerade as apostles of righteousness. Their master, of course, pretends to be an angel of light even as he goes about destroying believers. That is why many Christians are experiencing enormous hurt in so-called churches, and it is critical that every believer who cares about the truth should know the basic ways of differentiating true from false churches. And because false churches use half-truths, it takes a high level of the knowledge of the truth to recognize the deceptions bandied around using the name of God.

While varied gifts will be evident in apostolic churches, it is the work of apostles to ensure the churches maintain an overall focus that is Christ-centred and to give correction where need be. In so doing, the apostles must themselves ensure the origin of their own messages is Christ and nobody else.

The origin of the apostolic message

An apostle is a messenger sent by God. Christ said He had been sent by the Father, and in this sense He too was an apostle (Hebrews 3:1). As head over the church, Christ appoints apostles whom He sends to the church for the purpose of giving it guidance and correction, ensuring that it conforms to His will.

This means that an apostle whose focus is on the early church is misled, because it would appear that he has been sent by the early church rather than by God. The work of such an apostle would be to make every local church he interacts with conform to the image of the early church rather than the image of God.

The same argument applies for every denominational apostle, whose duty it is to ensure conformity to denominational doctrine regardless of whatever God may think about that doctrine. The only option open to an apostle who disagrees strongly with a denomination's doctrine is to quit that establishment.

To prove he was an apostle, Paul wrote about his relationship with Christ and how God had commissioned him, insisting that his message had not come from any man (Galatians 1:1, 11-12). Every true apostle receives his commission from Christ and is responsible only to God.

An apostle can refer to the message of another apostle, but this can be either for the purpose of affirming that message or giving correction. This is following in the footsteps of Christ, who was born under the Law but regularly referred to that law to give correction rather than concurrence. This same spirit is expected of later apostles when referring to the early church. If they only agree with the early church without hearing directly from God, they would be no better than the Pharisees and teachers of the Law who heard from Moses and nothing more. How then can they claim to be apostles?

The prophetic writings of the Old Testament reveal two main thrusts. The first was a desire for the people to obey the law given to them through Moses and to pinpoint areas of disobedience, asking them to renew their obedience of the law. The second was different, pointing to a greater righteousness of God and sometimes even scoffing at the people's legalistic obedience.

In Psalms 51:16-17, David says that God does not delight in sacrifices and burnt offerings, which were obviously commanded in the law. He points out that what pleases God is "a broken and contrite heart."

Isaiah spoke ill of the people's worship as simply empty words (Isaiah 29:13). Later, in Isaiah 66:1-4, he writes that it is impossible to build a house for God, going against the common thinking regarding the temple in Jerusalem as the house of God.

These kinds of non-conforming prophecies foreshadowed the coming of the new covenant, which focuses on inward transformation and on the people of God as His temple. These were liberating prophecies, departing from mere repetition of the law and drawing inspiration right from the heart of God.

Just as the prophets of the Old Testament heard God directly and gave correction even on the law given by Moses, true apostles must also hear from God directly and give correction on the early church teachings where necessary.

An apostle whose focus is Christ can truly give correction to other apostles and to the church in general. One whose focus is another apostle, even an apostle from the early church era, cannot hear any correction from God beyond the model he has lifted up; he cannot do better than the apostle he has adopted as his role model. The churches he is sent to will not benefit from any instruction higher than that given to the apostle he adores.

This would be akin to the Old Testament prophets looking up to Moses rather than God. The word given in such cases brought only oppression, while when they spoke from God's heart they gave life and frequently went against the law.

The Old Testament prophets were hardly popular, and more often than not they were persecuted and their messages rejected by people who had established their own traditions based on the law. That is still true today, when many sects have set up their own traditions that they associate with the early church's apostolic traditions.

Yet, the Old Testament prophetic writings that made a big difference did not seek the status quo of the burdensome law put in place by Moses in ages past. Rather, they looked beyond it into the future to the coming of Christ and the initiation of the new covenant.

Similarly, the apostolic focus of our day cannot be a return to the imperfect early church but, on the contrary, a preparation for the coming of Christ through perfection of the church as we see the Day of the Lord drawing nearer.

Differences between true and false churches

Neither a true nor a false church would be perfect in knowledge or practice. It is not such perfection that makes a church a true or apostolic reflection of God. This is not to despise knowledge; it is actually important that a Christ-centred church should seek— individually and collectively—to come to a proper understanding of what the Lord's will is and to move in obedience to such illumination. When such knowledge is coupled with obedience, it ensures victorious living that glorifies God.

The measure of a true church is to be found in having the life of Christ. Jesus must be its central theme, not just in words but in practice. Of course, Christ desires that we should all have a greater knowledge of Him, but the level we have attained at any particular time—our spiritual maturity, in other words—is not the determinant of whether we are truly born again or are a true church. A people who have just been evangelized and started meeting as a church will be as much a true church as those with a long tradition of 2,000 years. And a newly born-again individual is as much a child of the kingdom as one who has read the bible a dozen times.

Their readiness to hear the voice of Jesus makes true churches ready to alter their beliefs and practices once convicted by the Holy Spirit. This is not the case with false churches, where long traditions and vested interests come into play, hindering purification and correction by the Lord. This difference is discernible even when talking to individual believers, with those from true churches being more readily agreeable to new ideas than sectarian Christians—who must be careful lest they offend the official denominational line.

This readiness to accept new ideas is often mistaken for ease of acceptance of false doctrines. In actual fact, it is extremely difficult for false beliefs to penetrate true churches because of the fact that believers are well grounded in the word and ready to argue in defence of their faith. This is unlike the situation in false churches, where the word of one man or some sort of college of elders is followed unquestioningly.

We therefore find that in true churches, every belief or proposal must be properly grounded in the word, whose interpretation can of course be the subject of debate as people seek to discern the Lord's voice. In false churches, however, the basis for a belief or activity lies in approval by the leader or group of leaders, denominational teaching and tradition, and alternative texts that are often accorded a place that is superior to scripture.

This means that when God sheds light on an issue, it is easy for true churches to accept that word and apply it joyfully. In false churches, however, that word will quite often cause division that leads to even more sectarian splits. This is one of the major reasons why denominations end up begetting even more denominations.

Indeed, false churches are masters at imitating anything that has a veneer of success, however unscriptural it may be. It takes one false apostle to come up with a lie, such as "plant a seed if you want to succeed" (and by this is meant giving money to the false apostle, not planting a seed of love in the lives of other brethren) for half of sectarian Christianity to begin repeating this lie. Scams and falsehoods ranging from pyramid schemes and selling of anointing oil to philosophies of positive thinking that remove glory from God and lift up the supposed power of man are spread that way.

While no doubt intra-denominational as well as inter-denominational quarrels have been common throughout history, sectarian Christianity shares a legendary loathing for anyone who comes up with greater light, especially the true church. In fact, the common practice has been to brand those who have gained social acceptance "mainstream" while calling every group that differs from them or sheds new light on an issue a "sect". This loathing is evident among even the fathers of the Reformation, who gladly sanctioned the death penalty upon other Christians who held different beliefs and were promptly condemned as heretics—both by the Catholics and Protestants.

What exactly constitutes sectarianism? It is separation from the original faith. The issue, then, is to determine what true Christianity is, a deviation from which makes a group a sect. Genuine Christianity is not determined by numbers of followers. It is determined by the apostolic standard. Since that apostolic standard shows us that the true church only divides itself according to locality, any group that decides to separate on any other ground is automatically a sect. In a classic case of not seeing the log in their own eye, the world's largest sects are the ones that excel in giving others this tag.

The values of true apostles are different from those of false apostles. For instance, while true apostles see suffering as their mark and accept it gracefully, false ones insist on worldly riches and power as the distinguishing characteristic that portrays God's approval.

True apostles see the temple, Levitical priesthood, offerings and all other Old Testament practices as foreshadowing Christ. The focus of true apostles is the spiritual significance of these types and shadows—how they reveal Christ. False apostles, on the contrary, focus on the outward forms and teach their observance. These are twisted to suit contemporary circumstances, such as offerings being replaced with money, temples with church buildings, and the Levitical priesthood by the modern pastorate.

For instance, true apostles and churches will know that the temple in the New Testament is the body of believers. False apostles, by contrast, will insist on physical structures as "holy" houses of worship.

This mindset in the sects, moreover, deceives many into thinking that there are such things as holy places and days. The true church, of course, recognizes that it is believers who are holy, not inanimate objects, buildings or days of the week. Thus, a believer is with the Lord wherever he is and does not need to put up a hypocritical display of piety for a couple of hours every Sunday morning.

Indeed, the deception in counterfeit churches is responsible for bringing about the false dichotomy between the gospel and the secular. In actual fact, everything that a believer does is done for the Lord. That means there is no such dichotomy among the people of God.

As mentioned earlier, true apostles get their commission and instructions directly from God, and their interaction with other apostles is for the purposes of mutual encouragement, helping each other in the Lord's work, and mutual correction. When Paul became an apostle, he did not need any authorisation from the other apostles, because it was the Lord Himself who had commissioned him (Galatians 1:11ff). In Galatians 2, we find Paul even rebuking and correcting Peter, who was an apostle before him.

This is in marked contrast with false churches, where there are man-made hierarchies among apostles, bishops, pastors and whatever other cadres there may be and through which instructions flow downwards. All sorts of rituals are created for what they call ordination and thereafter any promotions to higher levels in the religious system. But even if men were to pour a full drum of anointing oil on someone's head and lay a thousand hands on him, that will not create an apostle; on the contrary, false apostles are the outcome of such efforts.

Moreover, true apostles help others to focus their attention on Christ rather than on themselves. Thus, Paul was not excited to find there were believers in Corinth who had decided to focus on apostles of their choice and some were saying, "I follow Paul," others, "I follow Apollos," and yet others, "I follow Cephas" (1 Corinthians 1:11-12). Paul in fact rebuked these believers for their worldliness, calling them "mere infants in Christ" (1 Corinthians 3:1). He expected them to focus their attention on Christ and not men.

Contrast this attitude of Paul with what happens in the denominational system. Every denomination shouts to everybody who cares to listen that they should come to them. Every spiritual leader who begins their own denomination seeks to have multitudes follow him or her. The various religious systems are focused on drawing attention to themselves, and more often than not on the individual at the top of the hierarchy. The attitude of adherents toward the spiritual leader will sometimes border on sycophancy. That is a distinctive mark of a false church.

Where the Spirit of the Lord is, there is freedom (2 Corinthians 3:17). True churches will encourage free participation by all present in exercising their priesthood. The work of the elders of the church is merely to encourage and steer this participation, ensuring that everything taking place is done for mutual edification. Nobody in such a gathering attempts to control the discussions, prevent any section of believers from freely participating, or dominate the proceedings. God reigns supreme and takes charge of the gathering.

False churches restrict this freedom with man-made rules and regulations. These rules spell out who is authorized to speak and when, the order of events at the gathering, the sitting arrangement, dress codes, etc. The total effect of these regulations is to restrict the freedom of believers to participate in the life of the church.

In order to clearly demarcate the clergy from the laity, false churches will insist on uniforms, special seats and titles. None of these is encouraged in genuine churches. Worshippers mix freely and efforts are actually made to ensure that everyone is made to feel equally valued. Use of spiritual gifts is encouraged by true churches, but these are used without resorting to titles.

The reason for this has to do with eliminating fear and encouraging participation. A policy that separates a certain category of Christians and lifts them up for special treatment discourages participation by the rest of the body of Christ. It encourages people to think of certain tasks, such as teaching of the word, as the preserve of religious professionals. It intimidates people and creates fear.

This is why the Christians described in the New Testament ministered without using titles. James also wrote against favouritism in sitting arrangements (James 2:1-4). Every effort is therefore made in true churches to remove fear and encourage mutual participation for edification. After all, God is love, and perfect love casts out all fear.

The relationship of true believers with God in true churches is one that is based on love, and it is this love that percolates down into their personal relationships. False churches, however, encourage an outlook of fear, and believers know of a vengeful God who is on the lookout for the slightest mistake to release his wrath. Again, this unfortunate perspective permeates into relationships among believers, creating hierarchies of human authority and fear-based obedience of denominational rules.

In true churches, love for God stems from what He has done for

His people: Delivering them from the clutches of the enemy, redeeming them to become His own people. Believers recognize that He has forgiven them all their sins—past, present and future—so that nothing can hinder fellowship with this glorious God. All participation is therefore geared toward giving praise to God for His wonderful love that has given His children rest, even as believers encourage one another in the walk of faith.

The situation in false churches is markedly different. Since a majority of sects give prominence to their rules and regulations, believers must continue working hard to please God and there is no rest for them. Sins must be continuously repented, either at the beginning or at some set point in the course of the meeting. Warnings are regularly issued to believers about the dire consequences of disobedience, even being abusively called "robbers" for not giving tithes in a sad but common misapplication of Malachi 3: 8-10. It is almost impossible for such believers to offer genuine, spontaneous sacrifices of praise out of hearts full of thanksgiving to a God whom they see as ready to strike them with curses any moment they slip over anything.

The dictates of love demand that all believers should seek the welfare of others in the family of God. That is why the bible exhorts Christians to love one another, instruct one another, bear one another's burdens, pray for one another, forgive one another, and do a host of other things to edify one another. A true church will excel in this, the focus being the good of all, especially the weak and timid.

A false church, however, turns this interactive focus upside down. There is an unbiblical clergy-laity divide, and the clergy are the ones to instruct, teach, pray for the laity, etc. The members of the laity, on the other hand, are supposed to financially support the pastor, bishop or whoever the members of these clergy are. The "one-another" actions that the bible urges upon all believers are therefore not mutual in false churches. The clergy is not called upon to support the laity financially, and neither can the laity teach and instruct the clergy.

When it comes to giving, for instance, while the funds raised by the early church of the apostles were mainly used to support the needy, in false churches these are used to support the clergy. True apostles do not make themselves a burden to others.

While the prerogative of God in granting spiritual gifts is respected in true churches, other considerations come into play in the case of false churches. Pastoring is taken to be a profession like any other, and one must have attended training in institutions acceptable to a particular denomination to minister as a member of its clergy. But because God is no respecter of persons, true churches will recognize that whatever gifts God wants to grant to people are not conditional upon any theological training or societal standing. In fact, theological training tends to hinder the operation of God's Spirit by making the trainees dogmatically-minded and fixed to specific denominational thinking.

Moreover, the exercise of spiritual gifts is discreet and used to edify one another in true churches. In false ones, however, spiritual gifts are for showmanship; the aim is to make a public display that attracts more people to the leader, guaranteeing increased power and finances. There will be no scruples of conscience when publicly exposing people's deepest secrets so as to gain the awe of television viewers in a display of supposed power.

In order to sustain the man-made system, false churches will go for one project after another—buying a bigger piece of land, construction of various buildings, putting up perimeter walls and beautiful gates, buying the pastor a vehicle, and endless others. True churches will have none of these, the focus being helping the poor. This is the same focus we find in scripture, where the funds raised by the apostles were used not on buildings and extravagant living, but helping widows and others in need.

Furthermore, in order to persuade people to continue contributing to an abusive and unbiblical system, false churches will shamelessly twist the word of God. This is done through a combination of half-truths and outright lies. Scripture is twisted at every possible opportunity to create an avenue for making money and ensuring total obedience to the denominational hierarchy.

For instance, Christians will be told that they ought to obey the Law of Moses with regard to tithing and first fruits, which in the modern context are said to be payable in monetary terms (as though there was no money at the time of Moses); they will not be told, however, why the pastor insists on only these two laws as important and makes no mention of the remaining 600-plus regulations.

The study of scripture in false churches is designed to ensure that the denominational doctrine on any matter is strictly adhered to. Open-mindedness is frowned upon, and that is why the clergy must attend select bible institutions where the "right" doctrine is taught. This is in marked contrast to the freedom found in true churches, where debate can be vigorous.

Because of this bigotry and related factors as discussed in this section, false churches tend to be extremely judgmental of others, both fellow Christians outside the sect and non-believers. They will not freely accept one who differs from them in doctrine, dress, or other circumstances. Some will readily censure one of their own for even visiting a different congregation. True churches, on the other hand, understand that believers are called upon to make a difference not just in the lives of fellow brethren but even among those whom the society considers outcasts. All are welcome to attend the gatherings of true churches without being judged. It is God who ministers as He wills.

The study of scripture in sectarian Christianity is rarely done so as to take the full context of the word of God into account. Proof-texting, which is the habit of isolating verses and interpreting them without getting into the context, is normal in false churches. The people are told what the pastor thinks they want to hear—something to encourage them, even if falsely, and in the process get even more money out of their pockets.

Moreover, in false churches the study of scripture rarely goes deep enough to discern spiritual significance. Obedience is at the level of literal rituals—not recognizing that God is not interested in ritualistic obedience but spiritual understanding. And so, false churches will preoccupy themselves with ritualistic activities and claim these are commanded. Their obedience is however selective; for instance, many will practice Holy Communion but not washing of feet, yet both are commanded if one wants to take a legalistic understanding. True churches will ignore ritual to the greatest extent possible.

Because of their deceptive focus on external factors rather than spiritual truth, false churches glorify miraculous signs, tongues, and other physical manifestations as a sign of God's presence. This deepens their deception the more. For instance, the Roman Catholic Church uses miracles as a proof that somebody is in heaven in their process of canonization. Many Pentecostals follow false apostles and are drained of their finances in their search for workers of miracles; a lot of them also think that Christians who do not speak in tongues are somewhat deficient, which is spiritual pride.

True churches do not entertain these deceptions. That doesn't mean God doesn't work miracles or grant supernatural gifts, but these are not the most important factor in our relationship with Him, and neither are spiritual manifestations greater than the fruit of the Holy Spirit in a Christian's life.

Obviously, the lack of solid biblical teaching in sects leads to a proliferation of false doctrines. The pastor will want to show that he or she is in control of every situation the believer may be facing, and the word of God will be twisted accordingly. If in sickness, the blood of Jesus will be called upon for healing—never mind that all biblical contexts show it was only meant for spiritual healing. If someone is embarking on a journey, the blood of Jesus will cover the roads and airports, even if nobody in the New Testament ever set such a precedent and the bible records no movement of the Spirit in that direction. Numerous such examples of the misuse of the scriptures can be cited.

A hierarchical command structure is key to false churches as it ensures unquestioning obedience to whatever the leadership wants. This can readily be seen everywhere within the denominational set-up. This is not the case with true churches. It is because there was no hierarchical system in the early church that the apostle Paul openly rebuked Peter in Antioch (Galatians 2:11-14). Today, it is virtually unheard of for a cardinal to rebuke the pope, or a priest in the Anglican hierarchy to rebuke a bishop.

This hierarchical system in false churches is found not just at the local church level, but even across churches. It is therefore common to find churches that are branches of other churches. Ultimately, all levels of authority report to the denominational headquarters.

This characteristic is completely alien to the bible, where we find that all local churches in the New Testament were independent entities. No true church can be under the control or direction of any other church or human spiritual authority. The only headship is that of Jesus Christ. When apostles visit local churches, their authority is persuasive; the local church has the final say, although they are encouraged to move into acceptance and application once convinced of the veracity of an apostle's message. No apostle can purport to exercise direct control of a local church, whose oversight should be left in the hands of local elders.

Such elders would exercise oversight through consultation with one another. A true church does not entertain single-pastor rule. Neither is anyone paid in order to minister to others, although believers may willingly support their own to excel in their God-given gifts. This may take the form, for example, of assisting a gifted singer to record his or her music, or an apostle who has been a blessing to them to travel to other churches. Whatever the case, all giving must be absolutely voluntary.

In arriving at decisions, moreover, false churches will rely on an individual's seniority within the hierarchy and the level of decision-making power accorded each position. Sometimes, decisions are also made by voting. True churches, on the other hand, recognize that the church was never meant to be a dictatorship where one person makes the important decisions, or a democracy where the majority have their way and the minority are left in pain. True churches make decisions through consensus.

It need not be emphasized that false churches fall far short of the biblical standard in these matters. Local churches are largely under the control of a single pastor, who reports to others in a hierarchical relationship. Moreover, believers are expected to materially support the local pastor and others higher in the hierarchy. These funds are sought using all sorts of manipulative manoeuvres, ranging from abuse of scripture to hurling abuses against those who don't donate according to the pastor's expectations. Preachers in these sects will generally encourage a mentality that the more the people give to them, the more God will grant them financial success.

The insistence on materialism and the allure of power have ensured that sectarian Christianity remains a perpetual theatre for power plays and destructive competition. The murders, fist fights and other ungodly activities that have marked the history of religious systems since the earliest days make for sad reading. True churches are about service, not wealth and power, and such behaviour is not given a chance.

Moreover, while sects will have people called pastors, apostles and so forth, these are totally different from the biblical description associated with these gifts. In actual fact, these are not titled positions or offices as used by false churches, but merely gifts (Ephesians 4:8). God's gifts do not entitle one to special privileges from other brethren, but are in fact a call for greater sacrifice on the part of the recipient. There is no gift from God that entitles anyone to silence everyone else in the church gathering and intimidate them to withdraw from active participation.

Many of the issues discussed in this chapter point to one other important fact: That while false churches seek to conform to the world around them, apostolic churches will do their best to remain true to their calling regardless of local circumstances. True believers and churches will not conform to the pattern of the world, but will instead seek to do God's will (Romans 12:2). The conformity of false churches to the ways of the world can be seen in various areas, for instance hierarchical relationships, titles and offices, physical structures, special dress, rituals, special seats, an equating of oratorical ability with spiritual power, and many others.

It is God who saves, not man. This statement is accepted as true by both true and false churches. But what are the implications of accepting that God is the one who saves? It means that other brethren have no choice but to accept the one whom God has accepted. Whether the person is rich or poor, white or black, of likeable character or not, the fact is that God has found it fit to accept that brother or sister. We must accept this person into the local church with no conditions whatsoever. That is what a true church does.

But what do we find in false churches? The sect will impose its own conditions for membership: You must register and perhaps get a membership card; you must pay your tithes regularly; you must attend catechism or doctrinal classes; you must attend Sunday services without fail, and perhaps notify the pastor whenever this is not possible; you must also be baptized according to the tradition of the sect, and undergo any other rituals that may be demanded of you.

Woe unto you if you ignore these conditions. You may find yourself isolated at your lowest moments, when you need comfort and help from the brethren. There is a clear policy about who deserves certain pastoral services and who doesn't. Questions that have zero significance—like who will preside over funeral services involving your family members if you do not live up to the sect's rules—take on disproportionate weight and become a source of group pressure.

False churches, in short, add their own conditions to God's grace in salvation, making God's gift appear burdensome and unattractive. They make it appear as though their self-imposed conditions are part of the package of salvation. Those who do remain in the sects cannot fully enjoy their new wine of salvation due to these conditions, while others opt to leave quietly, saddened by the heavy demands of what they thought was a loving God. Thus, these false churches aid Satan in his wicked schemes to make God seem unattractive, oppressing believers and discouraging multitudes from coming to the throne of grace.

The unity found in true churches is a one-ness in the Spirit, where the believers are united in love and may agree or disagree on non-core issues, while at the same time continuing to trust God for answers to questions where no agreement exists. The unity in false churches, however, is a unity in following the false apostle, regardless of how erroneous his or her teaching may be. That is what denominational statements of faith are supposed to do, anyway. That is why, also, any denomination's followers will normally come out strongly to protect their leader when under attack—regardless of whether the leader is on the right or wrong.

Because false churches insist on unity in outward matters rather than in the spiritual sphere, they tend to be intolerant of divergent opinions and where they have the power often resort to repressive measures. In the history of the church, these unfortunate measures against so-called heretics have included burnings on the stake, feeding believers to lions, massacres, confiscations of property, and general persecution.

Such bigoted and intolerant behaviour by false churches is the result of a false understanding of authority. True apostolic authority—such as that exercised by the apostles in the early church—is persuasive. Even though greatly disturbed by the false apostles who were opposed to him, Paul never called for their murder, or for a physical confrontation. He instead focused on spreading the word to those who would listen to him, warning them about the false apostles and false brethren. False churches are incapable of such authority and rely instead on manipulative methods—including the use of force—to assert their power.

Through encouraging exclusive thinking, false churches bring about a divisive "us versus them" mentality among Christians. When an Episcopalian Christian moves to a new area, he will not be seeking to find out whether there are Christians he can associate with near his new home, but whether these are Anglicans. If there are Christians but of a different orientation next door, he will conveniently ignore them and travel further afield in search of Anglican brethren. This cancer affects Christians across denominations and is one of the most serious problems of false churches.

A Christian whose focus is on Christ will find himself at home fellowshipping with other Christians wherever he goes. He will be seeking fellowship with followers of Christ, not Anglicans, Presbyterians, Pentecostals or any other shade of denominational followers. He will in fact resist becoming a part of any separatist or denominational grouping, but will cherish real fellowship even with denominationally-minded Christians to the extent possible. Of course, that does not mean going for a denominational monologue church service, but real sharing.

That brings us to the point that true churches do not separate themselves along any denominational lines. Neither Christ nor the apostles ever set up a denominational religious system, and for good reason. True churches only divide themselves on the basis of locality—one is a member of a local church on the basis of living in an area. Since Christ is as powerful in Nairobi as in Thika, a Christian who moves house from Nairobi to Thika should rightly meet for fellowship on a regular basis with Christians in Thika.

But suppose that such a Christian prefers moving from Thika to Nairobi, 40 km away, every Sunday morning and ignores all the well-meaning Christians on the way, what are we to make of this behaviour? First, it could be a sign of spiritual pride. Second, it is a show of ignorance about what a local church is all about. Third, it shows that there is something else, beyond faith in Christ and more important than pure faith to the believer, that is binding such a Christian to that congregation. It is a tell-tale sign of a cultic connection, membership of a false church.

This does not mean that members of true churches should not visit other true churches or fellowship with them. Actually, such interaction is to be encouraged. However, on a regular basis, the Christian will fellowship with other believers in his or her locality functioning as a local church.

Watchman Nee lists seven unscriptural grounds around which false churches separate themselves from the body of Christ: Spiritual leaders (hero worship); the instruments of salvation (people by whom one has come into God's kingdom); non-sectarianism (seeing sectarian Christians as not part of the body of Christ); doctrinal differences; racial differences; national differences; and social distinctions (*The Normal Christian Church Life*, pages 83-95).

The focus of true churches is always the welfare—spiritual and physical—of the whole church. False churches only care about the physical welfare of the clergy. The members of the laity are told that God will take care of their needs when they give their material substance to the clergy, which essentially amounts to a rip-off.

What are the measures of a successful church? A false church will point at three main things: The multitudes in attendance, the magnificence of physical buildings and projects, and the financial muscle of the group, which may also include political influence. These measures are of no consequence to true churches. The only true measure of success is obedience to the voice of the Master. Even if nobody listened to Jeremiah's message in the Old Testament days, with the people led by their priests instead preferring to throw him into jail, the prophet was hugely successful in God's eyes. Spiritual growth and obedience to God therefore take centre-stage.

Because of the materialistic focus of false churches, God's favour is measured by the amount of worldly possessions. When people in such sects pray for blessings, they have in mind jobs, money, land, houses and other possessions. The ones who are truly blessed are those who own these things in increasing measure. Such people will be accorded special treatment and offered leadership positions in various tasks and committees, even though spiritually they may be far removed from God. They will take the front seats in the "sanctuary" and be offered opportunities to "minister" to others. Their financial status and social positions are thus taken as a sign of God's approval, extending to spiritual work and oversight as well. But we know nothing can be farther from the truth.

Apostolic churches recognize that while God can and does provide financial provision to His people, the true measure of blessing is our submission to His will. Financial prowess is not a measure of God's anointing. In fact, for His own reasons, God will often allow those whom He uses mightily to suffer a lot of distress and trouble.

The book of Revelation was written by the apostle John when he was suffering in exile on the island of Patmos. The spiritual wealth in that book cannot be bought by any amount of gold and silver, yet John was at the time an old man languishing in exile far from home, with obviously no material possessions worth speaking of. Similarly, Paul was a mere tent-maker who was in and out of jail every so often; using the world's eyes, who would think such a person would have anything useful to say? Yet for centuries his letters, some written in prison, have been acknowledged as masterpieces that reveal to us the heart of God.

The suffering of God's people continues in many ways to this very day. Apostolic churches and believers can therefore expect to suffer ridicule, malicious gossip, loss of income and possessions, and sometimes outright persecution. This comes about because Satan's wrath is raised in opposition against them; wherever true believers turn, his power in the world system will be working to their disadvantage, even though many of those used by Satan may not realize what is happening. Moreover, just like in the days of Jesus and the apostles, other "believers" who claim to know God—particularly the false brethren in counterfeit churches—will often be instrumental in bringing about this suffering.

True churches therefore recognize that our task is to seek God and His righteousness, and that material riches will be given to God's people according to His will. They do not turn church gatherings into sessions for permanently trying to arm-twist the Lord to provide for their fleshly desires. That is what false churches do, not recognizing that the gathering is for the purpose of offering joyful sacrifices of praise and mutual edification of the brethren. Prayers for personal needs are not inappropriate, but can never be allowed to become the dominant and unending feature of the gathering in apostolic churches.

True churches are flexible and can meet wherever and whenever it is convenient, as the Lord directs. Since they are not fixated on numbers, regular meetings will tend to have smaller numbers of people—generally a number that can comfortably fit in a home. False churches are focused on having specific "sanctuaries" and the larger the numbers, the more they think the Holy Spirit is in their midst.

This flexibility by true churches extends beyond the local church gathering. In the same way that God has shown his readiness to manifest Himself in diverse ways in the course of history in order to minister both to those who are near Him and those who are far away, true churches and apostles easily adapt themselves to changing cultures and circumstances. This is why Paul writes that he had become, "All things to all people so that by all possible means I might save some" (1 Corinthians 9:19-23).

In so doing, believers do not change their beliefs and worship of God, but they bend over backwards in non-essential matters to accommodate those who might otherwise be hindered from coming to Christ. This is unlike in the sects, where there can be no flexibility unless the denominational headquarters determines it, most often as a result of pressure from adherents.

For instance, the Roman Catholic Church used the Latin mass across the world for centuries, and no deviation could be entertained. It took the decision of a church council to overturn this behaviour, which had basically appeared to elevate Latin into God's preferred language and to imply that worship in other languages was unacceptable to God. Yet not even the New Testament was originally written in Latin.

This rigidity in sects is what contributes to certain behaviour traits and attitudes in the world across denominations, such as taking crumbs of bread for what is generally called Holy Communion, dressing up on Sundays, encouraging near-similar clothes for the clergy, uniform greetings and linguistic expressions among adherents, and the use of multi-coloured windows for church buildings. One may easily think that even the manner of greeting one another determines your status in the kingdom.

But the word of God never makes demands on believers to give up their cultural diversity. All that is required is tolerance of one another's cultures. In fact, the mature believer is required not to become a stumbling block to the believer who imagines that food or dress is of any importance before God. If true knowledge of such matters is to be imparted, which would be a good thing, it should be done in love—but such knowledge should never become a condition for fellowship. Neither should believers be made to conform to a Jewish or any other culture outside their own worldview.

While freedom of thought and action in following the Lord is given a premium in true churches, false churches exercise control over the lives of believers. They will be told what proportion of their income to give for running of the religious organization, what to believe according to the doctrine of the denomination, and even how to dress when going to "the house of God." In many cases, pastors will discourage believers from reading literature that does not agree with the denominational doctrine lest their minds be polluted. Whenever travelling or relocating, the pastor will want to give advice on what denomination the believer should associate with in the new location. The Holy Spirit is given little room in this scheme of things, with the spiritual leader in full control.

When the total weight of sectarian thinking is brought to bear on the family, the resulting situation is sad indeed. Many families cannot worship together because individual members visit their sects of choice, a problem that would be non-existent if Christians were to meet according to the biblically-sanctioned model of locality. Regular night-long vigils away from home have caused untold problems between spouses. Financial oppression by sectarian leaders has left families that desired more of Jesus feeling disillusioned and heartbroken. Thus, the artificial divisions of sectarianism have served to bring disharmony in families, in neighbourhoods and between friends who ideally should be together.

At the end of it all, true churches will exhibit the redeeming power of God in people's lives, while false churches will bring about the bitter fruit of abuse and oppression.

Chapter 5

Restoration back to the imperfect early church

Both true and false churches have since the days of the Church Fathers claimed to draw their teaching and inspiration from the apostles and the practice of the early church as described in the New Testament. Indeed, the Roman Catholic Church claims to be a successor to the early church, and asserts (without any scriptural proof) that the apostle Peter was the first pope. Its claims to apostolicity lie partly in these claims of an unbroken succession line.

Protestant churches took the cue from the Catholics and made their own claims of following the practices of the early church. Presbyterians draw their practice of elder-ruled churches from the early church, as do Anglicans regarding bishoprics. Pentecostals, too, draw their teaching about Holy Spirit gifts from the practice of the early church. House churches have also been drawn into the fray, supporting their more relational practices from the example set by the apostles.

While it may be true that some of these and other practices are mentioned in the New Testament, picking a few teachings or practices from the New Testament is not sufficient to make a church apostolic. Neither does apostolicity have to do with trying to prove a physical unbroken line of succession. Rather, this is to be found in sharing the same spiritual walk that the apostles had, which is a focus on Christ and not men. In fact, where this focus leads one to conclusions that are different from those arrived at by the early church, that does not reduce the level of apostolicity. Even if an unbroken line of physical succession was to be proved by the Roman Catholics, for instance, the litany of scandals, murders and massacres associated with this particular denomination do not show an apostolic spirit but rather something dramatically different—and malevolent.

For a church to be apostolic, it must first of all be a true church and pass the test of the characteristics associated with true versus false churches as described in the previous chapter. The church must be assessed on a holistic basis and not just one or two points. Beyond this, however, the value of those practices that any church seeks to emulate from the first century church must also be assessed and the myth debunked that whatever the early church did was ideal and normative.

Numerous Christians have over the past few centuries become exasperated by the problems facing the church today and sought God for a solution. Starting with the Reformation, numerous solutions have been tested and put forward, many of which have helped in advancing the church a step closer to the truth and farther away from the abyss it had sunk into during the Dark Ages.

However, many of these changes have been only cosmetic. For instance, the break-up that resulted in modern Protestantism did not do away with the clergy-laity divide, and Catholic Fathers and Cardinals were simply replaced with Moderators and Vicars. A change in titles, while maintaining the division in the church, is no change at all. This kind of change, without uprooting the system, can only create small deceptive improvements but will still stifle the operation of God in denominational Christianity.

A rising number of Christians have sought to create greater changes by going back to the church of the apostles, the first century church. These well-meaning Christians have set their eyes on a return to the practice of the Christianity seen in the New Testament period of the apostles, which they argue is normative for the church.

The practices that are taken as normative and commanded by such groups will vary depending on interpretation. Stricter adherents will ask women to cover their heads and keep silent during the church gathering. They will also take wine and unleavened bread for communion, alongside a love feast. They conduct baptisms by immersion. Other regulations may include regular hours of prayer, such as at 3:00 am; segregation of men and women in seating arrangements; and a sprinkling of other Old Testament commands, for instance prohibiting women from wearing trousers as these are considered men's dressing.

Not all churches seeking a return to first century Christianity will follow all these rules, and the emphasis changes from one church to another. The only thing that is commonly held is the belief that the Christianity described in the New Testament is the ideal mode of Christianity that all believers should aim for. Indeed, even some denominations look for practices to emulate from the apostolic era, such as baptism by immersion and certain spiritual gifts, principally speaking in tongues.

But the underlying assumption that early church practice of the faith was normative and worthy to be emulated by all Christians cannot stand serious scrutiny. While the early church did much better than the contemporary one that is replete with false churches, it was by no means perfect. Thoughtlessly copying their beliefs and practices would result in an improvement from the current dismal situation, for sure, but will not lead to perfection. This means that the church today cannot hope to do better than the first century church if the latter is the model by which we will measure ourselves.

Moreover, even where the early Christians cannot be faulted, their practice of the faith was obviously adapted to their own socio-cultural situation. If they broke bread at their gatherings, that was because bread was one of their foodstuffs. Is the God we serve really so legalistic that we must accommodate the eating habits of first century Jews for our own worship to be acceptable to Him? A blind focus on returning to first century Christianity seems to suggest so, but the overall thrust of scripture does not support such a thesis.

When studying early church practices, therefore, the focus should be on the lessons we can learn rather than blind adherence to the rituals and practices of those early Christians. For instance, when we read that the early Christians broke bread at their gatherings, this can be taken to indicate that they had so much love among themselves that they shared food and drink at their meetings. Within our own cultural situations, we can share our foodstuffs together joyfully—be it rice, yams or potatoes. When we draw the lesson that we ought to share bread because that is what the early church did, we show that we are carnal and far from spiritual maturity.

It must not be forgotten that the church has gone through centuries of bitter debates, divisions and false teachings. The consequences are still with us, and there are deeply ingrained beliefs in today's Christianity that were not held by the early church. In going back to first century Christianity, many churches do not go deep enough to question these long-held assumptions. For instance, there was nothing like belief in a God who is a Trinity in the first century. The early Christians did not believe in such a thing as a God composed of several "Persons." A close scrutiny of apostolic texts also shows that the apostles did not hold the belief that the Holy Spirit was a different being from God the Father. Yet, these are beliefs that are unquestioningly held by many Christians today who are claiming to have returned to first century Christianity!

Therefore, not only does a return to first century Christianity fail to give us perfection, the efforts toward such a restoration are tainted by the current assumptions of believers. That calls for more drastic action that goes beyond restoration efforts.

Chapter 6

From Restoration to Perfection

God desires to receive all the glory from man, and that none should go to any other. In manifesting Himself in whatever form in the course of biblical history, His desire was to draw man closer to Himself.

There are those who have argued that the eternal purpose of God is to glorify His Son, Jesus Christ. This perspective is well argued in Frank Viola's book, *From Eternity to Here*. With the realization that the Son is not a different "Person" of God as taught by Trinitarians, however, it becomes apparent that God is seeking to bring glory to Himself. Since it becomes easier for human beings to identify with the man Jesus Christ, who was simply the very manifestation of the Father, when we behold Jesus we are essentially beholding God.

God is perfect, man is far from perfect. But for us to come anywhere near perfection, we must have a clear picture of the ideal that we aim for. And that is what the heavenly Christ beckons us to, because He wants a church without spot or blemish. So, what would the perfect church that reflects the image of our perfect God be like? And how do we get there?

Jesus was the perfect visible image of God, having been begotten of Him. God now wants the church to play this role, becoming His perfect image in the physical realm. He has empowered us for this role by giving us of his Spirit, which means that we have been adopted to become His sons and visible image on earth.

God has always desired to receive the undivided loyalty of His people. This is first and foremost through acknowledging Him as the only true God and worshipping Him only. But human nature being weak, we find that man has always veered into giving an ear to other voices that entice him to depart from worshipping and obeying God.

In the Old Testament, the people often turned to worshipping the idols and gods of the surrounding nations. In the New Testament, idolatry of this nature is rarely the case. What Satan has done, however, is still no less serious.

When Christians worship a Trinitarian God, it means they really do not know what they are worshipping. This is an advanced and hidden form of idolatry, where people worship non-existent entities under the deception that they are worshipping the true God. In that case, they are no better than the Israelites who mixed worship of Yahwe with that of Baal. That did not please God, who time and again sent his prophets to ask the Israelites to destroy the altars of false gods.

The truly apostolic church fixes its eyes on Jesus and does not tolerate the worship of false gods. Within the context of lifting to perfection the work of the early church, we can see that although the apostles did not clearly confess that Jesus is God, the church that desires perfection must do so. Not only this, the apostolic church must clearly state that there is no other God but Jesus, who is the Father and the Spirit. Whatever terminology may be used at any point in the bible to refer to Him, the fact is that there is no multiplicity in His being.

Moreover, the focus of every true church must be returned to Christ and removed from any apostle, past or present. The church must again learn to listen to the heavenly Christ rather than the first century apostles, whose every word must be held up against this high Christological standard.

At an individual level, any believer who justifies a point of teaching or practice on the ground that their spiritual leader believes it has fallen short of this standard. After listening to another believer—regardless of the social standing or perceived spirituality of that believer—every Christian has a responsibility to seek the scriptures and be personally persuaded that indeed what has been said is true.

But the matter gets more complicated when we read scripture and find that the words of a person in the bible, say an apostle in the New Testament, agree with what we have been told. Now, does this constitute a ground to say that the thing said and written is therefore God's will? The answer is still no, for God has not told us to remove our eyes from Christ and fix them on an apostle such as Paul, or Peter, or John.

This problem is only resolved when we understand at what level inspiration lies. As discussed in Chapter 1, the apostles and other giants of the faith mentioned in the scriptures were only human, just like ourselves, and had numerous weaknesses. The message of God is obtained by discerning the voice of the Spirit through the scriptures, sieving it carefully from the frailties of the people used by God. Essentially, this is what fixing our eyes on Jesus means.

Once this great gem containing God's message for the church has been obtained, we run with it for the benefit of ourselves and the church. Everything, including the writings of the apostles, is to be judged by this standard. Many times the prophetic and apostolic writings will measure up, but other times they will fall short. The church is to set its eyes on this ideal, and not a lower Petrine, Pauline or Johannine standard.

By looking to the apostle Peter, many preachers have justified their greed, saying that it was only Paul who worked for a livelihood. The implication is that it is okay for them to show less love for the flock and become predators simply because the bible appears to imply that some apostles did the same. They have even ascribed to Peter a higher position than the other apostles, using this to justify their own selfish desire for power among God's people. They can as well go the whole hog and begin separating believers in gatherings according to race or ethnicity, which is the hypocrisy for which Paul rebuked Peter in Antioch (Galatians 2:11-14).

Others who have focused on Paul as the "master builder" of the church have gone into the same error, taking wholesale the positive as well as negative aspects of Paul's teaching. This way, women have been silenced, the poor and oppressed told to shut up and be contented with their unfortunate situation, and prescribed dress codes—especially for women—have been introduced.

Perfection of the church now means that the time has come for the Bride of Christ to stop the fixation with the early church apostles and lift up her eyes to gaze upon Christ. God allowed the church to fix her eyes on the apostles for a time and for good reason: The church had descended into such a deep abyss that it needed to look to the early church so as to recover its sense of direction. God's ultimate desire, however, has always been for His people to fix their eyes on Jesus, the "author and perfecter" of their faith (Hebrews 12:2, NIV).

So, what does a church that has set its sights beyond the apostles and is headed for perfection look like? What are its hallmarks and characteristics? Many of these were mentioned in the discussion comparing true and false churches in Chapter 4 and do not need to be repeated at this point. Suffice to state that the standard of the true apostolic church is a complete Christological standard, and nothing below this absolute focus on God will do. It is a standard that judges everything from the words of Jeremiah to those of Paul, making every thought and argument obedient to Christ.

This kind of church becomes a fertile ground for the rise of true apostles, prophets, evangelists, pastors and teachers. Because these do not minister for any selfish gain, and neither are they keen on titles or social recognition, it is often easy to miss them out. A spiritual mindset, however, immediately makes one sharply aware of the wide range of spiritual gifts among the brethren within a short time. People will recognize the rich gifts of others in their midst, yet none is to seek their own glory or financial gain on account of the nature of their own spiritual gifts. The kind of vanity that leads to sectarianism as exhibited in denominationalism has no place in the gatherings of believers in true churches.

The distinguishing characteristic of God's people is love, and we know that where there is love no sectarian divisions can arise. It is by the measure of love that Jesus said the world shall get to know His followers. Whatever happens in the church must therefore pass the test of love. If there is any activity that shows a deficiency of love, then it deserves to be closely scrutinized whether it really is of God, or in what aspect the enemy may be operating to destroy God's work.

God is one, and this one-ness must be reflected in the unity of the church. This unity is spiritual, with believers everywhere expected to have the attitude and mind of Christ. The unity does not refer to organizational one-ness, which is what the Roman Catholic Church has claimed through the centuries. Neither does it refer to physical presence in one place, agreement on liturgical procedure, or even doctrinal consensus on every point. Rather, spiritual unity simply signifies a unity in the love of God and of one another. This unity is discernible in the daily lives of believers and how they arrive at decisions, solve problems and undertake various activities in their midst. The common goal of this unity is to glorify God in all situations affecting individual believers and the church.

Like any move of God, the transition from restorationist to what I call "perfectionist" is bound to be painful. Many sincere Christians who have sought to obey the Lord through a return to early church practices will be shocked to learn that their journey has been incomplete. These wonderful brethren, in their love for the Master, have embraced what they see as the New Testament model of church, even where some of their own freedoms have been curtailed.

Some of these brethren departed from their former religious organizations and systems in search of authentic Christianity, which they thought they had found in restorationist circles, house churches and other non-conformist groups. Many of them have found a sense of joy and peace in their current fellowships, which in a real sense do quite often represent greater light and truth than the denominations they left behind. It may now seem cruel to ask them to move again—not necessarily physically, but in terms of the knowledge of the truth—to a higher place that the Lord beckons us to, but that is exactly what must happen if God is to be glorified to the highest possible extent.

For those who have only joined such groups and were intent on settling down to enjoy their new-found fellowship in a modern replica of the early church, this is a wake-up call that their journey is far from over. They must move on before getting into a comfort zone, which will come with a thousand reasons why they must not move beyond that point.

For the many in false churches who have gained an acute awareness of the deceptions around them and are contemplating moving into deeper truth, an understanding of the nature of the perfect church makes their spiritual journey that much easier since they can once and for all focus on perfection, not having to make a stop-over at the restorationist phase. They have a full view of the journey before setting out, unlike others before them who had to make some stops on the way under the false impression that they had truly arrived.

Chapter 7

What shall we do?

The sincere believer is compelled to seek to implement every new-found nugget of knowledge and wisdom. When Peter preached to the gathered crowd on the day of Pentecost, the bible records the reaction of the listeners:

> When the people heard this, they were cut to the heart and said to Peter and the other apostles, "Brothers, what shall we do?" (Acts 2:37)

Since Christ desires a church without spot or blemish, it follows that it is the duty of every Christian to do everything in their power to achieve this ideal. Those whom Christ has entrusted with the task of equipping the saints have the great responsibility of unravelling centuries of confusion and helping the body of Christ to remove all spots and blemishes.

But because of the great increase in the numbers of false apostles worldwide, every Christian has the task, too, of learning the basics in discerning false teachings. The cleansing of the church involves the purification of every part of the body of Christ, which means every member must be involved in the task. Just as John the Baptist called on individual Jews to repent, so even today the remnant must play their individual roles in helping in the rebuilding of the church to fit God's ideal.

Of critical importance is knowledge of God's plan for the church. Without this knowledge, any efforts at rebuilding would be futile and at best incomplete. In the task of rebuilding, the focus must be on God's design and not any man's ideas, however lofty or impressive. Everyone who wants to be used by God in this work must therefore remove his or her focus from the teachings of denominations, religious leaders, the Church Fathers and all other human associations.

When it comes to the early church, it is important to develop discernment to know the will of God and separate this from the apostles' own cultural inclinations, doctrinal inadequacies, and other weaknesses. The early church can therefore serve as an important outpost in our journey of rediscovery, but should never be the ideal that Christians should aim for. The cultural situations, decisions and practices of the early church cannot be treated as infallible. The churches that have adopted early church practices have in many ways proceeded in the right direction, but they need to readjust their focus to see the greater glory of God.

Breaking with traditions is never easy, but that is exactly what Christians are called upon to do. Our desire for the truth of the word of God must be greater than our conformity with denominational traditions, love for leadership posts in the religious set-up, friendship with other church members and leaders with whom we have close relations, and every other consideration that may come up. The first challenge therefore has to do with the determination to make a clean break from the past regardless of all the odds that may come up.

Given the commercialization in counterfeit Christianity and its many worldly attractions, it is not to be expected that multitudes will be excited about the prospects of quitting false churches. Those who do take this leap of faith, however, will soon reap a harvest of spiritual rewards.

Withdrawing from a false church is never easy. The first and most difficult thing is for the individual to accept that he or she has indeed been deceived and is in a false church. When it comes to matters of faith, a majority of people are not easily persuaded that what they have believed all along could have been wrong. It is only by accepting the Lord's invitation to go to Him and "reason together" (Isaiah 1:18) that this demonic veil of deception can be lifted from the believer's mind. Once this happens, the journey begins.

There will be visits from the sectarian leadership and members to find out what has happened, and Christians who have decided to take a new course will need to be firm and honest about the decision they have taken. There will be all sorts of negative rumours and malicious gossip doing the rounds. Ostracization is not far-fetched, and old friends will quickly dissociate themselves and have nothing to do with the Christian who has left their sect. Loss of income and source of livelihood is a possibility. In extreme situations, more severe physical persecution may also result. The kingdom of darkness goes into overdrive to oppose any Christian who has by faith quit the counterfeit church and is bent on discovering the truth.

The Christian who has embarked on the journey to please God rather than men should not be discouraged by all these setbacks. He should continue to show love to all—including those in the sects—without compromising his principles. He should also seek out other Christians who have embarked on this journey for purposes of mutual encouragement. God is faithful and many are surprised, upon leaving the denominational setting, to find that there are many other Christians walking with God outside the religious establishment.

Caution is however necessary. Satan is a master deceiver and one may find false churches that appear, on the face of it, to have received the light to walk outside the religious establishment. Upon closer scrutiny, however, God's Spirit will reveal to the attentive believer the deceptions in such a group. Domination of the gathering by an individual who is primarily acting like any denominational bishop and building his or her own kingdom while giving participatory church lip service should raise suspicion. Any attempt to dominate others betrays a sectarian bias.

True church is not just about moving out of organized religion. That is only the first step. There are many house churches, for instance, that are more of micro-denominations transplanted into private homes than true churches. Actually, the place of meeting is of little significance even though a home—where a suitable one is available—offers an ideal environment.

Everything should be kept as simple as possible. There is no point of leaving one religious organization to join another. The aim is to leave the religious organization to participate in the life of the true church. Vigilance should therefore be maintained to protect simplicity, and attempts to set up an elaborate organization should raise questions about the ultimate aim of the group's leadership.

This does not mean that it is wrong for a believer to belong to registered groups, or even to help in their establishment. However, financial support groups or any other organizations should be recognized as such and not called churches or confused with the body of Christ. The church has no need of worldly authority to go about its business, and can only inform authorities of a gathering in the same way that a family meeting bringing together extended relatives would do. Of course, all this would be dependent on local circumstances; even where it may be prudent to get some sort of registration due to official demands, this should never form the basis of spiritual authority.

The registration certificate would only be for the purpose of showing local officials who may visit and nothing more—it should never be the basis of division or membership, which remains locality. The assumed name of the group should not be taken to be a real name and flaunted around, since only locality counts—hence the church in Corinth, Ephesus, Juja, Thika, Ruiru, and so forth.

The believer will develop his spiritual antennae as he navigates through the maze of false churches that stick out like a sore thumb while pretending to be advancing the interests of the true church. He will also come across true churches that are deficient in some points of teaching and practice. That should not be a hindrance to fellowship in love, especially on non-core issues such as dress and foodstuffs.

As churches faithfully organize themselves on the basis of locality, God will provide all the gifts that each of these churches need. This may not happen immediately, but will surely come to pass as God's power becomes evident in the gathering. Moreover, visits between churches within easy reach of one another should be encouraged; this provides a basis for further encouragement and accountability.

Needless to say, the word of God must be the guiding light of every believer and true church. The best safeguard against false doctrines and the deception of false churches and apostles is to encourage believers to immerse themselves in the study of God's word. It is by the living word that the church will be purified, setting the stage for Christ to return for His bride.

Having removed every spot and blemish, the church can then call out, "Come, Lord Jesus." To which he responds, "Yes, I am coming soon." Amen.

Bibliography

Alexander, T.D. and Rosner, Brian S., *New Dictionary of Biblical Theology*, InterVarsity Press, UK., 2000.

Anthony, E.C., *Considering Worship*, US, 2008.

Atkerson, Steve (Editor), *House Church*, New Testament Reformation Fellowship, US, 2008.

Berkhof, Louis, *Systematic Theology*, The Banner of Truth Trust, US, 1958, 2005.

Bonhoeffer, Dietrich, *The Cost of Discipleship*, Macmillan Publishing Co., NY, US, 1959.

Bramsen, P.D., *One God One Message*, Rock International, SC, US, 2007.

Brauch, Manfred T., Abusing Scripture: The Consequences of Misreading the Bible, InterVarsity Press, US, 2009.

Brown, Michael L., Revolution in the Church: Challenging the Religious System with a Call for Radical Change, Chosen

Books, US, 2002.

Bubeck, Mark I., *The Adversary: The Christian Versus Demon Activity*, The Moody Bible Institute, Chicago, US, 1975.

Bubeck, Mark I., *Overcoming the Adversary: Warfare Praying Against Demon Activity*, The Moody Bible Institute, Chicago, US, 1984.

Bunyan, John, *The Pilgrim's Progress*, Whitaker House, PA, US, 1973.

Carrier, Marc, The Gospel According to Jesus: Unwrapping Centuries of Confusion, Kingdom Expansion Series, Values-Driven, 2010.

Cole, Neil, Organic Leadership: Leading Naturally Right Where You Are, Baker Books, US, 2009.

Culver, Robert Duncan, *Systematic Theology: Biblical and Historical*, Christian Focus Publications Ltd, UK, 2005.

Davidson, Ivor J., *The Birth of the Church: From Jesus to Constantine, AD 30- 312*, Volume 1 of The Monarch History of the Church, Monarch Books, Oxford, UK, 2005.

Dickason, C. Fred, *Angels: Elect & Evil*, Moody Press, US, 1975.

Elwell, Walter A., *Evangelical Dictionary of Theology*, Baker Academic and Paternoster Press, UK, 1984, 2001.

Erickson, Milard J., *Christian Theology*, 2nd Edition, Baker Academic, US, 1998.

Fee, Gordon D. and Stuart, Douglas, *How to Read the Bible for All Its Worth*, Zondervan, Michigan, US, 2003.

Fortenberry, Jack, *Corinthian Elders*, Bridgepointe Publishing

Company, Brandon, 2008.

Green, Michael, *Evangelism in the Early Church*, Hodder and Stoughton, London, UK, 1978.

Grudem, Wayne, Systematic Theology: An Introduction to Biblical Doctrine, InterVarsity Press, UK, 1994, 2005.

Harlow, R.E., *Christ in the Old Testament*, Everyday Publications Inc., Canada, 1990.

Harlow, R.E., *Christ in the New Testament*, Everyday Publications Inc., Canada, 1995.

Harlow, R.E. (Ed.), *God the Son*, Everyday Publications Inc., Canada, 1974.

Hendriksen, William, *The Gospel of Matthew*, New Testament Commentary, The Banner of Truth Trust, UK, 1973, 1989.

Hill, Jonathan, The History of Christian Thought: The Fascinating Story of the Great Christian Thinkers and How They Helped Shape the World as we Know it Today, InterVarsity Press, US, 2003.

Ing, Richard, *Spiritual Warfare*, Whitaker House, US, 1996.

Josephus, Flavius (Transl. Whiston, Wiilliam), *The New Complete Works of Josephus*, Kregel Publications, MI, US, 1999.

Kraft, Charles H., *Confronting Powerless Christianity: Evangelicals and the Missing Dimension*, Chosen Books, 2002.

Kreeft, Peter and Tecelli, Ronald K., *Handbook of Christian Apologetics: Hundreds of Answers to Crucial Questions*, InterVarsity Press, US,

Lloyd-Jones, D. Martyn, *Authority*, InterVarsity Press, London, UK, 1958, 1976.

Marshall, I. Howard (Editor), New *Testament Interpretation*, The Paternoster Press, US, 1992.

Mwangi, Isaac, *Poisoned Well of Tradition*, Mina Chariots Publishers, Nairobi, Kenya, 2013.

Nee, Watchman, *The Normal Christian Church Life: The New Testament Pattern of the Churches, the Ministry, and the Work*, Living Stream Ministry, Anaheim, US, 1980, 1994.

Oliana, Guido, *The Gift of Religious Life: Sparks of Lectio Divina*, Paulines Publications Africa, 2002.

Patzia, Arthur G., *The Emergence of the Church: Context, Growth, Leadership and Worship*, InterVarsity Press, 2001.

Pearse, Meic, *The Age of Reason: From the Wars of Religion to the French Revolution*, The Monarch History of the Church, Vol. 5, Monarch Books, 2007.

Pierce, Ronald W. and Groothuis, Rebecca Merrill, *Discovering Biblical Equality: Complementarity without Hierarchy*, InterVarsity Press, US, 2005.

Price, Hope, *Angels: True Stories of How They Touch Our Lives*, Pan Books, 1993.

Prime, Derek, *Pastors and Teachers: The Calling and Work of Christian Ministers*, Southside, UK, 1989.

Prior, David, *The Church in the Home*, Marshall Morgan and Scott, UK, 1986.

Ramm, Bernard, *Protestant Biblical Interpretation* (Third Revised Edition), Baker Books, US, 1970.

Reid, Daniel G. (Editor), *The IVP Dictionary of the New Testament: A One-Volume Compendium of Contemporary Biblical Scholarship*, InterVarsity Press, Illinois, US, 2004.

Renwick, A.M. and Harman, A.M., *The Story of the Church* (Third Edition), InterVarsity Press, Leicester, UK, 1958, 1999

Robertson, Edwin, *Bonhoeffer's Heritage: The Christian Way in a World Without Religion*, Hodder and Stoughton, London, UK, 1989

Snyder, Howard A., *New Wineskins: Changing the Man-made Structures of the Church*, Marshall, Morgan and Scott, London, UK, 1975.

Thoman, Roger, *Simple/House Church Revolution*, Appleseed Publications, US, 2008.

Turner, Max, *The Holy Spirit and Spiritual Gifts Then and Now*, Paternoster Press, Cumbria, UK, 1996.

Viola, Frank, *From Eternity to Here: Rediscovering the Ageless Purpose of God*, David Cook, US, 2009.

Viola, Frank, Pagan Christianity: The Origins of Our Modern Church Practices, Present Testimony Ministry, 2002.

Viola, Frank, Reimagining Church: Pursuing the Dream of Organic Christianity, David C. Cook, Colorado, US, 2008.

Viola, Frank, Rethinking *the Wineskin: The Practice of the New Testament Church*, Present Testimony Ministry, 2001.

Virgo, Terry, *Restoration in the Church*, Kingsway Publications Ltd, Sussex, UK, 1985.

Walker, Andrew, Restoring the Kingdom: The Radical Christianity of the House Church Movement, Hodder and Stoughton, London, UK, 1985.

Warren, Rick, *The Purpose Driven Church: Growth Without Compromising Your Message & Mission*, Zondervan, MI,

US, 1995.

Willmington, H.L., *Willmington's Guide to the Bible*, Tyndale House Publishers, Illinois, US, 1981, 1984.

Websites:

biblicalunitarian.com

revelations.org.za

ABOUT THE AUTHOR

Isaac Mwangi is a Kenyan author and journalist. Born into a Catholic family, he later moved into a Pentecostal denomination for several years before leaving it to follow Jesus outside the religious establishment. He is now part of the growing house church movement.

He has written one other book, *Poisoned Well of Tradition: Baptism and worthless rituals in the church*. He lives with his family in Juja near Nairobi.

Website: www.minachariots.com

Printed in Great Britain
by Amazon.co.uk, Ltd.,
Marston Gate.